Getting Libraries the Credit They Deserve

A Festschrift in Honor of
Marvin H. Scilken

Loriene Roy
Antony Cherian

The Scarecrow Press, Inc.
Lanham, Maryland, and Oxford
2002

SCARECROW PRESS, INC.

Published in the United States of America
by Scarecrow Press, Inc.
A Member of the Rowman & Littlefield Publishing Group
4720 Boston Way, Lanham, Maryland 20706
www.scarecrowpress.com

12 Hid's Copse Road
Cumnor Hill, Oxford OX2 9JJ, England

British Library Cataloguing in Publication Information Available

Library of Congress Cataloging-in-Publication Data Available

ISBN 0-8108-4455-9 (pbk. : alk. paper)

♾™ The paper used in this publication meets the minimum requirements of
American National Standard for Information Sciences—Permanence of
Paper for Printed Library Materials, ANSI/NISO Z39.48-1992.
Manufactured in the United States of America.

Contents

iii

Preface

Loriene Roy and Antony Cherian

In its "special end-of-the-century history issue" of December 1999, *American Libraries* listed the one hundred most influential librarians of the century. They chose only those who lived and died in the twentieth century, including pioneer figures Andrew Carnegie and Melvil Dewey and more contemporary leaders such as the University of Illinois at Urbana-Champaign's Hugh Atkinson and West Virginia's Fred Glazer. Marvin H. Scilken is number seventy-nine in this alphabetical roster. The eighty-word entry identifies some of Scilken's accomplishments as an editor, publisher, author, advocate, mentor, and professional colleague.[1]

This volume pays tribute to Marvin H. Scilken. A traditional festschrift is a gathering of essays to honor a scholar. This festschrift, however, is part edited volume of essays, part autobiography, and part biography.[2] By gathering this variety of contributions we hope to commemorate Scilken through his professional actions and beliefs. Our title, "Getting Libraries the Credit They Deserve," was the campaign slogan Scilken employed during his 1991 campaign for President of the American Library Association (ALA).

The festschrift is divided into three parts. Part I consists of five chapters dedicated to the public service philosophy Scilken held dear. Lisa Bier places the role of public library advocacy in the sweep of public library history. Scilken spent much of his time trying to convince the public of the importance of public libraries and trying to convince librarians of the importance of focusing on the user. In chapter 2, Katherine Flowers explores Scilken's belief in putting patrons—and especially readers—first.

Regan Robinson's contribution in chapter three first appeared in *Librarians Collection Letter: A Monthly Newsletter for Collection Development Staff.*[3] Talking to Robinson, Scilken described how public library directors can create a collection that responds to patron needs. Dr. Joanna Fountain, in chapter 5, describes how Scilken's views of collection development were based on his conviction that library catalogs be developed with the user first in mind. Scilken tempered his respect for the catalog with common sense. Dr. Loriene Roy's chapter on ALA Council illustrates how Scilken's influence extended beyond his own Orange (New Jersey) Public Library. She tells the story of life as an ALA Councilor-at-Large and all the power, small glamour, and hard work it brings.

In the three chapters of part II we hear Scilken's own voice in three different ways. The first is an excerpt of an extensive interview of Scilken by Joseph Deitch in December 1992. Mr. Deitch takes us on a tour of the Orange Public Library with its renowned director and number one fan. We are sorry to convey that Mr. Deitch passed away before the completion of this book. His son Edward Deitch, a producer and writer for "NBC Nightly News" conveyed that he read portions of this chapter aloud at his father's memorial service as testimony of Joseph Deitch's love of writing, libraries, and books.

Four hundred of Scilken's quotable phrases are compiled in chapter 7, a reference work within the festschrift. Most of these quotations were gathered from the pages of the U*N*A*B*A*S*H*E*D Librarian (U*L), primarily from Scilken's editorial asides in the "Author's Mumblings" and "Notes" sections of the newsletter. Chapter eight reprints the content Scilken contributed to the ALA ballot in spring of 1997, the fifth and last time Scilken ran for election as Councilor-at-Large. Its reproduction here allows Scilken to reintroduce himself as a library professional.

We gathered nine tributes in part 3. Chapters 9 and 14 are contributions from the two people who knew Scilken best, his widow, Mary (Polly) Scilken, and his older sister, Dr. Marjorie Scilken-Friedman. Polly Scilken's biographical entry is a succinct summary of Scilken's professional contributions. She reminds us also that he was a loving family man. Dr. Scilken-Friedman introduces us to Marvin Scilken as a boy using super-human strength to make his point. Perhaps this story explains why Scilken did not type. Dr. Scilken-Friedman also writes letters to the New York Times and, in honor of her brother, she signs these letters with her maiden name.

Dr. Dan O'Connor contributes a balanced view of Scilken as a professional colleague. It is the biographical entry he prepared for the forthcoming revised edition of the distinguished Dictionary of American Library Biography.[4] Jack Forman reflects on Scilken's legacy of influencing through mentoring. Peggy Sullivan's chapter provides insight into Scilken's work as an ALA Councilor from her perspective as former ALA President. Mitch Freedman revised the tribute he gave Scilken from the floor of ALA Council the morning Councilors learned of Scilken's death.

Chapters 15 and 16 reprint two of Karen G. Schneider's "Internet Librarian" columns from American Libraries. The earlier column, "Desperately Seeking Marvin," is testimony to Scilken's influence as a mentor. "The Elements of Marvin," full of praise for the U*L, is a tribute to the power of professional communication.

The last chapter was prepared by recent library school graduate Matthew Mantel. Mantel relates how he discovered Marvin H. Scilken and how Scilken will continue to influence the next generation of information professionals.

Holly King's bibliography lists two hundred of Scilken's publications plus nearly sixty references to letters he wrote to a variety of publications. She also lists forty references to articles about Scilken. This compilation is selective rather than comprehensive.

We invite you to join us in celebrating Marvin H. Scilken, maverick unabashed librarian, through his work, through the words of those who knew him, loved him, and respected him, and through the earnest efforts of a number of new information professionals who will carry his work forward into the new century.

Our portion of the proceeds from the sale of this book will be donated to the scholarship established in Scilken's name at Pratt Institute's School of Information and Library Science.

We are grateful for Polly Scilken's guidance and encouragement through the preparation of this book. Peter Larsen pitched in to help edit and format chapters when we most needed his assistance. Our families and friends waited patiently for us to complete the project. We appreciate their patience and support, especially that of Raymond J. Mooney, Owen Mathias Hunter, and Danny Fletcher.

Notes

1. "100 of the Most Important Leaders We Had in the 20th Century," *American Libraries* 30 no. 11 (December 1999), 38–46, 48.

2. Edwin S. Gleaves, "A Watch and Chain and a Jeweled Sword; Or, The Graveyard of Scholarship: The Festschrift and Librarianship," *RQ* 24, no. 4 (Summer 1985): 466–73.

3. Regan Robinson, "Selection with Scilken," *Librarians Collection Letter: A Monthly Newsletter for Collection Development Staff* 5, no. 2 (July 1995): 1, 3, 6.

4. Donald G. Davis, Jr., ed. *Second Supplement to the Dictionary of American Library Biography* (Englewood, Colo.: Libraries Unlimited, in press), s.v. "Scilken, Marvin H. (1926–1999)."

Part I

A Meaningful Professional Life

Chapter 1

Library Advocacy

Lisa Bier

Library advocacy can be a slippery term. It is not just marketing or public relations, although marketing and public relations are effective tools to lobby on libraries' behalf. Since there are as many rationales for the American public library as there are citizens, advocacy has taken many divergent, even conflicting directions. To some, public libraries will always first be repositories of human knowledge. We create them to protect the resources within their walls. To others, libraries champion the public's freedom of access to information. Libraries provide the public with materials to pursue lifelong learning. For those who work in libraries, library advocacy includes yet another element. It aims to establish the rights and improve the working conditions of library staff.

These competing perspectives do share certain core values. Perhaps a working definition of library advocacy could be to convince the tax-paying public and the tax-allocating government to establish and support free public libraries. Advocates stress that although libraries do not reap a financial profit, they benefit communities in ways that cannot be measured by the bottom line.

EARLY ADVOCATES FOR THE PUBLIC LIBRARY

Libraries have existed in this country since early colonial days, but the general public only had limited access to reading material before the establishment of free public libraries. In the mid-eighteenth century, entrepreneurs established circulating libraries from which people could borrow a book for a fee.[1] Social

3

libraries, also called subscription libraries, existed for those who fit class and gender restrictions and could afford to join.[2] Some owners of large mills or factories provided libraries for their workers.[3] Private academies and colleges had libraries that were not open to the public.[4] Churches and Sunday schools sometimes had libraries of limited size and scope.[5] Occasionally towns housed collections of donated books for borrowing, but they rarely had funds to create a permanent home for the books, let alone to establish a budget for book purchases, to hire a staff to oversee the collections, or to maintain reading rooms.[6] In general, working-class Americans and their families had little time, less opportunity, and few materials for reading.

The first free public libraries were often established through the efforts of idealistic individuals or groups. They believed that citizens deserved free access to reading materials. Their motivations, however, varied. Some thought libraries could provide moral improvements.[7] Others felt the need to keep people off the streets. Envy of another municipality that had established its own library was a common—if less lofty—incentive.[8] Across the board, these libraries intended for "all citizens" still served only white patrons and rarely admitted people of color.

The earliest true public libraries appeared in New England. Several towns have compelling claims to the title of first American public library. As library historian Jesse Shera explained, this disparity can be attributed not to "ignorance of historical fact," but to problems in defining the term *public library.*[9]

The citizens of Franklin, Massachusetts (one contender for the country's first public library) received a surprise from their town's namesake when they wrote Benjamin Franklin in 1785, requesting money for a meetinghouse bell. He instead sent them a number of books.[10] The earliest library open to the public that received some municipal support was that of Salisbury, Connecticut. It was created in 1803 when Caleb Bingham, a Boston bookseller, gave a gift of 150 books intended for the youth of Salisbury. Caleb Bingham recalled how in his own youth he "longed for the opportunity for reading, but had no access to a library."[11] In New Hampshire in 1833, a plan to establish a public university fell through, and the town of Peterborough used the money that the state returned to them to fund a library instead.[12]

Nicholas Marie Alexandre Vattemare planted the seeds of the Boston Public Library in 1841. Vattemare, a French ventriloquist, encouraged the various private social libraries of Boston to unite under one roof. His personal goal was to have a library in the United States with which to share international materials, books, and government documents. Vattemare's idea sparked the interest of many of Boston's civic leaders, and after thirteen more years of negotiations regarding control and organization of the facility, the city government agreed to support the library.[13]

Some of the earliest advocates for public libraries in the United States were the women's clubs that formed all over the country in the wake of the Civil War. Upper class women met in these clubs in order to foster enrichment in their own lives. With ample leisure time and few obligations to the financial support of their own families, they formed reading groups and organizations that focused on civic improvement. They felt the need to morally uplift others they believed were less fortunate than they. They hoped that promoting literacy might improve the lot of these "less fortunate," and the enriching environment of the library was one means to their end.[14]

The women's clubs collected donations of books and held fundraisers. They created the first traveling libraries that circulated to towns in outlying areas. They then worked to create permanent libraries open to the public.[15] These women's clubs often had to lobby male politicians for financial support and permission to create libraries in their districts.[16]

Representatives of the women's clubs were many of the first applicants for grants from Andrew Carnegie, another early advocate of library services for the public.[17] Not formally educated, Carnegie was an archetypal self-made man. He believed the library was a place where the motivated worker could find a lifetime's worth of education. In his youth, Carnegie had benefited from the generosity of one Colonel James Anderson, a man who had opened his own home library to the workingmen of Allegheny, Pennsylvania.[18]

Carnegie used his immense wealth to fund 1,689 library buildings in 1,419 communities in 47 states, the District of Columbia, Puerto Rico, and elsewhere worldwide.[19] The first of Carnegie's libraries opened in 1889 in two of the Pennsylvania towns that were home to his huge steel mills and thousands of his workers. The library grants program continued to fund library building projects until 1919. Carnegie required that cities and towns provide the building site and promise to support the library financially at an annual rate of 10 percent of the total amount of the grant. Since many of his wealthy contemporaries believed charity only provoked and prolonged the problems of the lower classes, he insisted that his grants provided a means of self-education for the motivated individual.[20] Similarly Carnegie's stipulation that the town provide continuing financial support for the library meant that the town took responsibility for its long-term success.

Although Carnegie's money funded the construction of the library building and not the book collections within them, it is his legacy that the presence of a municipal public library is a minimum requirement of the American standard of quality of life. The temple-like buildings that Carnegie financed in towns all over the United States fostered the symbol of a library as a center of civic development, growth, and improvement. Yet it must be remembered that, in truth, every public library probably has its own tale of an individual who worked for its existence, an individual who made an immense commitment to the town's intellectual well-being.

The American Library Association (ALA) was founded in 1876, with the express intent of creating a professional organization of librarians dedicated to "promoting the library interests of the country, and of increasing reciprocity of intelligence and good will among librarians."[21] Three years later Melvil Dewey penned a less unwieldy motto for the organization, "the best reading for the largest number at the least cost."[22] The association's membership consisted of upper-class, educated white male administrators of larger public libraries—and a few women—who took on faith that they knew exactly what the best reading for the largest number was. For many years librarians assumed they knew what was best for their readers, and many libraries avoided fiction for its purportedly deviant properties. A 1926 ALA publication written in celebration of the organization's fifty-year anniversary still held this position, dramatically and nautically stating that, "no one knows better than librarians that the reading they do provide is but a mere drop in the vast sea of print, pouring down upon us and threatening to inundate us, the undertow of which is so powerful that at times we are swept beyond all reach of the refreshing and stimulating currents of true literature and of the gentle influence of things which are honest and of good report."[23]

Other significant achievements of the association mentioned in the 1926 report included international affiliations with librarians in other countries, the establishment of permanent facilities and staff for the association, the provision of books for overseas soldiers during World War I, the development of library schools, advances in professional literature, and the establishment of library buildings in communities throughout the United States. Conspicuously absent, however, were the campaigns for which ALA is best known today.

LIBRARY ADVOCATES TODAY

Today, ALA focuses its efforts on five key action areas: recruiting people of color to the profession, continuing education, promoting the library as a democratic institution, intellectual freedom and anticensorship, and twenty-first century literacy for library users. ALA also has an office dedicated to library advocacy activities.

ALA's Library Advocacy Now! campaign responds to the public's lack of awareness of services provided at libraries as well as their difficulty grasping the concept of library advocacy. *The Library Advocate's Handbook*, published by ALA's Public Information Office, lists library trustees, Friends of Libraries groups, library users, community leaders, and library staff as among those who should consider themselves library advocates.[24] The *Handbook* outlines an action plan for creating a positive image for the public library in a time when many Americans feel that the home computer and the World Wide Web render the public library obsolete. The *Handbook* provides sample responses to questions such as "isn't the Internet going to put public libraries out of business?" and helps libraries create a plan to explain effectively to elected officials, voters, taxpayers, and others why the public library is still a necessity for modern life.

ALA's Washington office lobbies in the halls of government on behalf of the people's libraries. Staff at the Washington office monitor legislation relevant to library issues. Issues include, but by no means are limited to, telecommunications, copyright, appropriations, privacy, filtering, and Internet governance. The office provides briefs and press releases on current issues and their relevance to libraries, and offers tips on contacting members of Congress and using grassroots lobbying to effect positive change for libraries. The Washington office also organizes National Library Legislative Day, an annual event that allows library supporters the opportunity to visit Congress en masse and express their views on library legislative issues to their senators and representatives.[25] Most state library associations also organize a Library Legislative Day.

Libraries have another advocate in Washington, D.C. The current First Lady, Laura Bush, is a former librarian and teacher with a Master of Library Science

(MLS). Many library organizations have embraced Bush in the hopes that her high profile and powerful connections will be a benefit to the country's libraries. Bush has a history of supporting libraries, and in September 2001 her successful Texas Book Festival became the model for the Book Festival at the Library of Congress, complete with live broadcasts on C-SPAN. Paradoxically though, her husband supports much of the legislation that the ALA Washington office is actively campaigning against. For example, while ALA sees Internet filtering as a dangerous obstacle to the individual's right to freedom of access to information, a campaigning George W. Bush stated, "You bet there's things the government can do. . . . We can have filters on Internets where public money is spent. There ought to be filters in public libraries and filters in public schools so that when kids get on the Internet, there's not going to be pornography or violence coming in."[26] Bush has not worked as a librarian in two decades, during which library issues and technology have changed dramatically. So her silence on these issues may be attributable to a lack of understanding. Yet, Mrs. Bush appeared to have a very different viewpoint than her husband, when in announcing a new initiative to recruit librarians to the profession, she stated, "There's nothing quite like a trip to the library. Whether you choose a casual stroll down the aisles of books or a speedy trip along the information superhighway, libraries will allow you to journey as far and as wide as your imagination will go."[27] The danger lies in the possibility of the country and the government viewing her as a spokesperson for what is best for the nation's public libraries when she may not represent the views of the majority of librarians at all.

The generosity of Bill Gates toward libraries in the late 1990s has been equated with that of Andrew Carnegie a century ago, and the mouth of his gift-horse has been studied equally thoroughly. Just as many Americans saw Carnegie as a robber baron whose money was ill-gotten in the first place, some see Gates's funding of computers for public libraries as suspect and self-serving. The Gates Library Foundation, now the Bill & Melinda Gates Foundation, has provided grants to purchase computer equipment in many underfunded library systems throughout the country. Although his gift certainly further raises the profile of Microsoft Windows platform computers, its effect on the next generation of computer users remains to be seen.

Friends of Libraries organizations are another source of support. Many libraries rely on their Friends group volunteers for basic tasks, such as shelving and processing books. For even more libraries, the presence of the Friends group allows the library to offer special programs and services far beyond the limitations of its own staff and budget. Local Friends groups organize some of the most ingenious forms of library advocacy. The national group, Friends of Libraries USA (FOLUSA) assists local Friends groups by providing guidance and ideas, and lists "promoting the development of strong library advocacy programs" as one of its four main goals.[28]

Library advocates can also be found in unexpected places. Nicholson Baker, who is not a big fan of library-weeding policies, is one of the greatest library advocates to come along in a while.[29] Although Baker has brought many librarians' dirty laundry into the public view in *New Yorker* articles and in his book *Doublefold*, the fact that he is writing about libraries and communicating his interest to the general public is a major achievement in itself.[30] In *Doublefold*,

Baker calls upon the general public to take an interest in the newspaper collections of libraries and in the actions of the librarians who maintain these collections.[31] As the saying goes, "there's no such thing as bad publicity."

Anything that raises public interest in the activities of libraries can lead to positive developments. Another example of the positive effects of negative publicity is that attention conservative media figure Dr. Laura Schlesinger brought to the issue of Internet filtering. Before her campaign for tighter control of public-access workstations in public libraries, many people were probably unaware of the technological flaws and political biases of Internet filtering.[32]

Television and movies, occasionally thought of as the archenemies of genteel libraries, host some surprise advocates. *The Simpsons* wholeheartedly mocks libraries, portraying them as deserted spaces staffed by blinking, grey-bunned old lady librarians, with screeching bats flying out of rarely opened card catalog drawers. But Lisa Simpson repeatedly solves the family's problems at the library, using library resources. *Buffy the Vampire Slayer* relies on Giles the librarian for his reference work—value added vampire eradicating data.[33] *The Mummy* movies use a librarian for both plot and comedic devices without relying on the shopworn stereotype of the uptight librarian. Several years ago, Parker Posey's *Party Girl* gave library school students if not a role model, at least a truer reflection of themselves and the changing spectrum of librarianship.

ADVOCACY FOR LIBRARIANS

Advocacy for those who work in libraries has been often overlooked. As one of the original "women's professions," library science, along with teaching, nursing, and social work, has always had to fight low salaries, professional disrespect, and annoying stereotypes. Librarians now are experiencing unprecedented popularity thanks to the field's association with high tech developments such as database programming and Web site design. Recent articles in the *Boston Globe*[34] and the *New York Times*[35] predicted an impending shortage of librarians over the next decade. Their twenty-first century skills are in such demand that librarians are finding jobs that are better paying and more rewarding outside of the traditional library field.

Before this mass media acceptance, which incidentally has not rocketed every librarian into the top tax bracket, librarians fought hard for respect and equitable compensation. The transformation of library work from labor to professional status has been a long and storied road.

ALA, successful in many other areas of library support, has never made a major campaign of improving working conditions and salaries. ALA provides the accreditation for schools that offer the M.L.S. degree but does not do enough to promote fair salaries for those who work hard and take out student loans in order to earn the degree. Many but not all libraries require librarians to have the M.L.S., but ALA does not have the power to enforce this stipulation or even offer guidelines for staffing ratios. Many municipalities are not aware of the crucial role of the professionally degreed librarian in providing services, and ALA could do much more toward educating policy makers about this issue.

There have been many library workers, therefore, who felt that the benefit of the professional association was less than tangible. What good was a self-imposed sense of professionalism, if salaries didn't provide a living wage? The first union for public library employees was the Library Employees' Union of Greater New York, founded by militant suffragist Maud Malone. Malone was known for aggressive pursuit of rights for women, and occasionally her actions—such as loudly interrupting male politicians in the middle of campaign speeches—caused her to be ejected from public places and even arrested.[36] In 1917, she decided to apply her activism to organizing a union of library assistants and librarians but not of administrators. The unions sought equal opportunity and pay for women in all levels of library employment and better salaries for all. The union frankly opposed the professionalization of the library field on grounds of elitism and convincingly argued that while men worked for financial reward, women were expected to be satisfied by the moral rewards and social benefit of their work.

The union also pointed out that few male library directors had the library degree, which was considered a necessity for female library assistants. Malone's direct and aggressive tactics were ahead of her time. Her union caused much discussion in the New York newspapers and at ALA but was not generally embraced by librarians in the area.

The debate did not end then. Some librarians and library administrators continue to see unions as ill suited to the needs of a profession, but some librarians have benefited greatly from the representation offered by unions.[37]

As libraries began to expand their roles as providers of reading materials, librarians realized the limitations of free reading material in combating societal problems. Libraries began to offer services such as outreach to immigrants, foreign language collections, bookmobiles, literacy tutoring, and employment centers. For a while, it seemed like the library could play a role in improving just about every aspect of American society. In the 1970s, Marvin Scilken published *GO, PEP, AND POP! 250 Tested Ideas for Lively Libraries*, a collection of promotional, public service, and community relations ideas for public libraries. The two librarians who authored this guide suggested that librarians plant community gardens, hatch sea monkeys, and borrow human body parts from local hospitals for hands-on biology experiments. Consider this recommendation to libraries: "Be a temporary home for someone's pet. Boa constrictors, monkeys, myna birds all need care when their owners are moving from one place to another or are going away on vacation."[38] Today's overworked and litigation-sensitive librarians have understandably backed away from this universal responsibility. Being the nation's source of reading material, champions of free access to information, stalwarts against censorship, and wizards of technology is enough for most librarians.

The role of the public library in the American community has never stopped changing. If the last decade has taught us anything, it is that the public library will never reach stasis. The challenge is not to define the library but to recognize that its roles and possibilities will never be set in stone. For it to thrive and remain relevant the library must reflect the changing society it serves.

Still, the one factor that will not change is that libraries will always need individuals who fervently believe in the library as a vital institution. It was the vision of advocates such as these that propelled libraries' new developments, transforming yesterday's distant dreams into today's basic necessities, whether it was a permanent building or Internet access for the public.

Notes

1. Haynes McMullen, *American Libraries Before 1876* (Westport, Conn.: Greenwood Press, 2000), 137.

2. McMullen, *American Libraries Before 1876*, 65–66 .

3. McMullen, *American Libraries Before 1876*, 139–40.

4. McMullen, *American Libraries Before 1876*, 106.

5. McMullen, *American Libraries Before 1876*, 83.

6. Theodore Jones, *Carnegie Libraries Across America: A Public Legacy* (New York: John Wiley & Sons, 1997), 17.

7. Jesse H. Shera. *Foundations of the Public Library: The Origins of the Public Library in New England 1629-1855* (Chicago: University of Chicago Press, 1949), 217.

8. Jones, *Carnegie Libraries Across America*, 17.

9. Shera, *Foundations of the Public Library*, 156.

10. Shera, *Foundations of the Public Library*, 205.

11. Shera, *Foundations of the Public Library*, 158.

12. Shera, *Foundations of the Public Library*, 161–66.

13. Shera, *Foundations of the Public Library*, 173–81.

14. Paula D. Watson, "Founding Mothers: The Contribution of Women's Organizations to Public Library Development in the United States," *The Library Quarterly* 64, no. 3 (1994): 233–35.

15. Watson, "Founding Mothers," 239–42.

16. Watson, "Founding Mothers," 243.

17, Watson, "Founding Mothers," 254.

18. Jones, *Carnegie Libraries Across America*, 5.

19. Jones, *Carnegie Libraries Across America*, 130.

20. Jones, *Carnegie Libraries Across America*, 6.

21. George Burwell Utley. *Fifty Years of the American Library Association* (Chicago: American Library Association, 1926), 12.

22. Wayne A. Wiegand, *The Politics of an Emerging Profession: The American Library Association, 1876-1917* (Westport, Conn.: Greenwood Press, 1986), 23.

23. Utley, *Fifty Years of the American Library Association*, 28.

24. Linda K. Wallace, ed. *Library Advocate's Handbook* (Chicago: American Library Association, 2000).

25. American Library Association. "Welcome to the ALA Washington Office," http://www.ala.org/washoff/ (21 Jan. 2002).

26. Norman Oder, "Filter Issue Goes Down to the Wire," *Library Journal* 125, no. 19 (November 15, 2000), 16.

27. American Library Association. "American Library Association Applauds Presidential Proposal to Fund Librarian Recruitment, Training," ALA News Release. Jan. 9 2002, http://www.ala.org/news/v8n1/librarian_recruitment.html (21 Jan. 2002).

28. Friends of Libraries USA. "About FOLUSA," http://www.folusa.com/html/about.html, (15 Jan. 2002).

29. Andrew Richard Albanese, "Double-Edged: Is Nicholson Baker a Friend of Libraries?" *Library Journal* 126, no. 11 (June 1, 2001), 103–4.

30. See Nicholson Baker, "The Author vs. the Library," *New Yorker* 72, no. 31 (October 14, 1996), 42–56 and Nicholson Baker, *"Deadline," New Yorker* 76, no. 20 (July 24, 2000), 58–61.

31. Nicholson Baker, *Doublefold: Libraries and the Assault on Paper* (New York: Random House, 2001).

32. Patrizia Dilucchio, "Dr. Laura Targets the New Sodom: Libraries," *Salon.com* 30, no. 8 (27 May, 1999), http://www.salon.com/tech/feature/1999/05/27/dr_laura (21 Jan. 2002).

33. GraceAnne DeCandido, "Bibliographic Good vs. Evil in *Buffy the Vampire Slayer*," *American Libraries* 30, no. 8 (September 1999): 44–47.

34. Jerry Ackerman, "Demand, salaries rise for librarians," *Boston Sunday Globe* (January 14, 2001), M2.

35. John W. Fountain, "Librarians Adjust Image in an Effort to Fill Jobs," *New York Times*, 23 August, 2001, 12(A).

36. Catherine Shanley, "The Library Employee's Union of Greater New York, 1917-1929," *Libraries and Culture* 30, no. 3, (Summer 1995): 235–64.

37. Tina Maragou Hoverkamp, "Professional Associations or Unions? A Comparative Look," *Library Trends* 46, no. 2 (Fall 1997): 232–44.

38. Virginia Baeckler and Linda Larson, *GO, PEP, AND POP! 250 Tested Ideas for Lively Libraries* (New York: U*N*A*B*A*S*H*E*D Librarian, 1976), 37.

Chapter 2

Putting Patrons First: Increasing Circulation with In-House Marketing and Promotion

Katherine A. Flowers

Conventional wisdom suggests that libraries increase circulation by attracting new users. As a result, librarians spend a considerable length of time contemplating nonusers and devising strategies to draw them in. The literature supports this mind-set with frequent marketing features and success stories about libraries that have launched campaigns to develop a digital presence or attract the Starbucks crowd. Marvin Scilken took a different view. While Scilken never denied the power, or even the necessity, of marketing, he believed that public relations would only in very rare cases bring new, steady users to the library.[1] Instead he argued that cajoling citizens to become library users could actually hurt the library's image, especially if services were already spread too thin or if the new users quickly became entangled with fines.[2] Scilken's argument calls for caution. Not every new patron drawn in by a gimmick will have a satisfactory experience. If our true goal is to encourage consistent library use, there may be a better way to do it. Marketing, in Scilken's view, should improve the library's image and raise its profile within a community. It should not focus solely on bringing in new users.[3] His way to increase circulation was to concentrate on improving service for the users we already have.

This philosophy challenges librarians. We are not likely to forget about outreach. We know what we have to offer, and it is our mission to extend service to those who need it the most. Many of the articles in the *U*N*A*B*A*S*H*E*D Librarian* reflect this ethos. However, core users already committed to the public library are the group most vital to its success. Philip M. Clark's 1998 study of the Ocean County Library System in New Jersey suggests that a relatively small number of "high-intensity borrowers" who describe themselves as "compulsive, addicted readers" are responsible for a significant percentage of the library's circulation.[4] In this scenario, a single satisfied patron can have a startling effect on a library's circulation statistics. Of course, the same is true for a patron who has had negative experiences in the library. This notion may make librarians uncomfortable, but we would be unwise to overlook it. We have an obligation to serve the community as a whole, but we are also bound to listen to our individual users.

With these thoughts in mind, this chapter will explore the possibility of increasing circulation through in-house marketing and promotion. It will focus specifically on improving service for the patrons we have now. As Scilken wrote, "Real readers search our shelves desperate to find good reads. We should make it easy for them."[5]

Promoting the Books on the Shelf

Perhaps the most powerful tool for selling or circulating books is the arrangement of the collection. Bookstores work hard to create an inviting atmosphere that encourages their customers to linger and browse. Their books aren't confined to the shelves. They are propped on stands and piled on tables. Music plays in the background, and an overstuffed chair lurks around every corner. Ceilings tend to be high, and the lighting is soothing. It is impossible to walk from one section to another without pausing because something intriguing, out-of-the-ordinary or maybe just fun to look at captures the eye. This collection invites, even demands, browsing. The same collection can frustrate a user looking for a specific title or needing information about a particular subject. The bookstore's bibliographic control is weak, but its collection is just inventory after all.

Libraries often approach their collections from the opposite direction. Their bibliographic control is tight and regulated. Each book is assigned to its space in the collection, and the collection itself is carefully balanced among patrons' demands for research, entertainment, and education. Shelves are crowded, tables are reserved for study, and the pace is often more frantic than relaxed. This atmosphere is not entirely unexpected, nor is it necessarily a bad thing. As Jack Alan Hicks explained before the Illinois Library Association in 1994, libraries and bookstores are different types of institutions with very different goals. By focusing on those differences libraries can actually become stronger.[6] Bookstores only become a threat if libraries change their focus to selling books instead of providing free reading material and information. Libraries can, however, learn a great deal from the merchandising of bookstores. A collection better suited to browsing does not take away from the library's primary goal, nor does it need to make finding information any more difficult. The key is to find a middle ground between the bookstore's glorious chaos and the library's classical precision.

To answer to this call, the *U*N*A*B*A*S*H*E*D Librarian* is filled with segments about how to make the stacks feel friendlier. Scilken himself advocated "classifying to merchandise." He explained that in the Orange (New Jersey) Public Library he created a Dewey number (942.085'71) just for books about the current Royal Family and then placed all of these titles the histories, biographies, and gossip together on the shelf.[7] Tactics like this one promote browsing and make sense to users. More importantly, this sort of arrangement saves the user time. In *The Measurement and Evaluation of Library Services*, Sharon L. Baker and F. Wilfrid Lancaster wrote, "The ideal library is organized so that its patrons expend minimum effort to obtain access to bibliographic materials when they need them. This is because patrons, consciously or unconsciously, will weigh the cost of a service against the benefits of using it."[8] If so, then ease of access means everything. The goal then becomes designing a layout that promotes browsing and serendipitous discovery without sacrificing bibliographic control. Scilken's modification to the catalog suits this aim well. But if dabbling in nonfiction classification leaves us uneasy, there are a number of other practical suggestions to make our collections more accessible.

The first way to merchandise is through fiction separation. Typically, genre distinctions in the fiction collection can be made in two ways—either by labeling the spines of books or by physically dividing books into different sections. Baker's 1985 research suggests that either approach will increase circulation and that physical division can have remarkable results in larger libraries.[9] The way this strategy works is simple. Divided or labeled fiction guides browsers directly to the type of books that most interested them. This arrangement simplifies decision-making and encourages serendipitous discovery through browsing. It may also cause problems. In 1990, Amanda McGrady of the Onslow County Public Library in Jacksonville, North Carolina, wrote about putting her library's fiction back together, citing patron complaints, space limitations, and an increased workload.[10] These concerns are very real, especially for a small to medium sized library.

Larger libraries may encounter obstacles as well. Physical division requires space, and it can also lead to difficult choices. Jeffrey Cannell and Eileen McClusky, for example, ask where to shelve Stephen King's *The Eyes of the Dragon*.[11] Would horror fans be interested in the book simply because of the author, or would it be better to shelve the book with other titles in the fantasy genre? A similar question arises now that Robert Parker has written a western. We have to consider whether avid fiction readers are primarily fans of an author or of a genre. The answer, of course, is both. Scilken suggested shelving all of an author's books together or making shelf notes explaining that additional titles by an author may be available in another section.[12] The library's public access catalog would also need to include notes regarding shelf location. Depending on the size of the library, this cross-reference may be too much work. Baker recommends that large libraries should physically separate fiction and that all libraries should make use of spine labels.[13] Scilken reminded his readers that no prudent retailer would risk trying a customer's attention by inter-shelving mysteries and westerns.[14]

Weeding can also serve to make the collection more accessible to readers. Space, after all, is at a premium. We must make room for new books and ensure that patrons can easily examine the titles on our shelves. Of course, a library's stacks will always be more crowded and perhaps less attractive than those found in a bookstore. As Hicks reminds us, libraries stock the retrospective fiction, comprehensive biographies, and reference titles that the bookstores do not.[15] Still it is not necessary to drown in the previous decade's midlist of mediocre fiction.

Merle Jacob suggests that libraries formulate an action plan for weeding fiction that incorporates the institution's mission, the collection's goals, and the needs of the community.[16] Book condition should also be a consideration. Reading a yellowing paperback with brittle pages requires a certain investment, and unless its content is exceptional, few readers will make the effort. Still, not all genres should be weeded according to the same guidelines. Scilken suggested weeding mysteries, which are perhaps the best book investment a library can make (and science fiction sparingly).[17] Romance fiction, on the other hand, becomes dated very quickly. Because of these distinctions, it pays to set different cutoff dates for genre fiction and to consult avid readers for guidance. In spite of its difficulties, weeding is well worth the bother. Carefully removing certain titles from the shelves can help to make the stacks more inviting and give the library a bit more room to maneuver.

A final factor creating browser-friendly stacks is the physical placement of materials. It requires more effort to examine a book placed on a high or low shelf than it does to glance at a title placed at eye-level. If we are serious about mitigating the effort required to browse our stacks, we should consider shelf placement. Intensive weeding and acquiring additional shelving can increase accessibility to books on library shelves. Baker suggests periodically shifting materials on the shelves so that readers will be drawn to different titles.[18] Facing some books outward or stacking duplicate titles one on top of the other may help also. Even small changes in spacing can break up the rows and catch the browser's attention.

Libraries may never replicate the browsing collections of bookstores, but to do so would be a mistake. It would mean offering the public fewer resources and concentrating on the new and hot at the expense of the timeless. Much of our value is in our noise and our bustle and our crowded shelves. Nevertheless, if we value our users and are serious about helping them find what they want, then a few modifications in the stacks can go a long way. These changes may mean sacrificing some of last decade's midlist fiction or increasing the amount of time we spend creating signs, labels, and other finding aids, but these changes will also increase our circulation.

Book Lists, Displays, and the New Readers' Advisory

While retooling the stacks and placing a greater emphasis on browsing is an important first step in marketing the collection, it is still essentially a background change. Libraries must use other more overt merchandising tactics to round out service. In truth, displays and book lists are more than simple merchandising. They are an essential service. Readers' advisory today doesn't take place at a desk or even face-to-face between the librarian and patron. As Baker writes in "A Decade's Worth of Research on Browsing Fiction Collections," during a time when library resources are stretched thin, we need to "manage our existing resources as effectively as possible."[18] In part we need to improve the fiction collections we already have by making them more accessible to browsers and by encouraging successful selection.[19] We do this through arrangement, but even more so through book lists, displays, and conversations between patrons and library staff. This is merchandising, but it is also readers' advisory.

A good book list is the perfect marriage of readers' advisory and merchandising. If it is well designed, it will not only lead the reader into new browsing territory, but it will have a lasting impact on circulation. It will create a demand for older obscure, or otherwise overlooked titles. Recognizing their utility, the *U*N*A*B*A*S*H*E*D Librarian* has published a number of comprehensive book lists on topics as diverse as building self-esteem and planning a family reunion. But for a book list to be truly successful, it must reflect both the library's collection and the community it serves. Chris Rippel of the Central Kansas Library System explains that we must be wary of frustrating users by promoting hard to find titles. It may be best instead to concentrate on author lists that promote lesser known writers within a genre or to follow the "if you like . . . , try . . ." format. Only list individual titles when multiple copies are available.[20] The content of the list should also fill a very specific information need within the community. Librarians can determine this need by keeping track of patron interests or even current events. Marian S. Edsell cautions against choosing a topic that is too obscure but at the same time reminds librarians not to underestimate their patrons.[21] Nonfiction book lists dealing with difficult subject matter can be just as popular as the current roundup of western romances if they address timely topics that appeal to patrons. Finally, a book list must not only point out the best or the most readable books in the collection, it must also in some way make the patrons' browsing experience more convenient. Readers may, therefore, want annotations or blurbs that they can glance over at home. Librarians also need to ensure that the list is easily understood, and the list itself should be colorful, humorous, or somehow noticeable. This sort of preparation takes time, but the results are worth the effort.[22]

While book lists are unquestionably a form of readers' advisory, displays can run the gamut from merchandising to genuine guidance. Sometimes they are little more than a collection of flashy covers. Other times they are made up of carefully annotated selections intended to introduce a topic or broaden a readers' knowledge. Studies show that both minimal and elaborate displays are effective. In *Readers' Advisory Service in the Public Library*, Joyce G. Saricks and Nancy Brown describe creating carefully organized thematic promotions specifically for readers' advisory. These displays are easily accessible and contain twenty to thirty books that readers know librarians have endorsed. The displays are simple, often on carts, with plainly lettered but catchy signs.[23] These promotions allow the reader to make choices within a carefully culled set, narrowing the selections available and guiding the reader to the best the collection has to offer.

Conversely, Que Bronson of the Metropolitan Washington Library Council advocates designing displays specifically to catch readers' attention. She suggests conducting an analysis of traffic areas and then setting up entrance, up-front, end-of-aisle, point-of-purchase, and open-floor displays.[24] Bronson's displays are full and say little about selection. Instead she focuses on technique, carefully elaborating on the advantages of pyramids over floor displays and the need to keep zigzag shelving well stocked. Bronson's displays do move books but at the same time readers' advisory has all but vanished from the promotion. Perhaps libraries should keep both schools of thought in mind and practice creating displays that offer a little of each. After all, not every display has to elaborately promote the best of the collection. In some cases simplicity may be best. Baker, for example, suggests simply placing a catchy sign over the carts of recently returned items.[25] Each display should somehow make selection easier for the patron.

In the end, the essence of readers' advisory, whether traditional book recommendation by a librarian or in-house merchandising of the collection, is best understood through examining it in application. Gimmicks, guesswork, and sound theory create the mix of factors that bring a reader in touch with a good book. Keeping this in mind, what follow are some unique and practical promotional ideas and marketing tips from the *U*N*A*B*A*S*H*E*D Librarian*.

Customer Reviews and Ratings

One of the most deeply entrenched library taboos is writing in books. Marking up a text another person might read is considered selfish, almost sacrilegious. At the same time we value the opinions of other readers enough to join book clubs, read reviews, and chat in bookstore aisles. Scilken recognized this contradiction and left space in the back pages of his library's novels for customer ratings.[26] The system includes a stamped "Good/Bad/So-So" column and space for reader initials. This promotion sparks interest, encourages debate, and fosters connections among patrons. It also allows users to get away with something a little unexpected. Promotion that invites reader participation and anonymous or low-risk sharing, is widely recognized in educational circles but has received little attention in library literature.

Buy Lots and Lots of Paperbacks

Library consultant Robert Smith suggests buying multiple copies of popular titles and buying lots of paperbacks.[27] If we want to increase our circulation, we need to make sure that our collections reflect what our patrons want to read. If paperback romances circulate, then it is time to invest in more. The same is true for bestsellers and other genre fiction. As for what to do with all of these books once the rush is over, Smith simply suggests using them in displays.[28] Although the strategy may seem mundane, the truth is that paperbacks are a relatively safe investment. If they are weeded, the library has not lost much. One of our primary goals, after all, is to give patrons access to as many books as possible, when they want them. Investing in paperbacks and multiple copies of bestsellers is one way to do that.

"Would You Like Fries with That?"

Due to the realities of staffing and funding, it is unlikely that most patrons, on a casual trip to the library, will speak with an actual librarian. Instead they will browse, check out displays, and occasionally pick up a book list. But most of all, sometimes patrons will converse eagerly with pages and the staff at the circulation desk. To ask our staff to serve their customers and promote the institution places a tremendous burden on them. Still, one consultant suggests training the staff in readers' advisory.[29] But another contributor simply advises the staff to ask marketing questions to remind patrons of the many services available at the library. Some suggestions are, "Did you find what you were looking for?" "Do you need any videos for the weekend?" or even "Did you know that we have CD's now?"[30] It is an elegant solution. At once, patrons feel valued and the library promotes its services.

"The Bestseller Club" and "Hot Titles"

Charging for services can be a minefield, but in limited cases it may help both the library and patrons get what they want. A prime example of this exchange is the Chandler (Arizona) Public Library's Bestseller Club. The club allows patrons to purchase a bestseller at a discounted price and then donate it to the library once they have read it. Patrons get the books they want to read quickly, and the donation becomes a tax deduction.[31] This program does require a substantial monetary investment from the patron as well as a great deal of effort on the library's part. Another more accessible promotion is the Traverse Area (Michigan) Library District's HOTS program. This campaign allows users to rent popular titles for a limited time. The prices are reasonable one dollar for a two-week rental and most of the titles are also available for free in the regular collection. Patrons who don't want to wait can take advantage of HOTS.[32] Both scenarios offer an opportunity to respond to patron demand with limited risk.

"Books You Might Have Missed"

Mimi Morris of the Dayton and Montgomery County Public Library writes, "Philosophically, I am convinced that people will take older books either for the first time or to re-read old favorites if they are reminded that the books exist *and* we make it very accessible for them to pick up."[33] She keeps a display of older books in a prime location with a sign such as "Novels (or Biographies) You May Have Missed." The display is effective in part because of the implicit recommendation, but also because it offers a second chance.

Pushing Book Lists

Rippel maintains that if book lists are going to be successful, they must be handed to patrons.[34] The patron is already so besieged by the library's books and bustling activity that he or she is unlikely even to notice the rack of pamphlets near the circulation desk, much less to see the carefully designed book list on the second row from the bottom. Expecting the patron to take a booklist leaves too much to chance. Therefore, we need to become more assertive in distributing lists. Rippel suggests stocking lists at the circulation desk and then placing them inside books that patrons check out.[35] This technique would also allow for a certain amount of targeting. Patrons who like Louis L'Amour, for example, could receive a list featuring today's western writers. Other patrons on the same day might receive lists of hot new romances or ethnic cookbooks. This approach ensures that titles on the list will receive at least a glancing exposure every time a patron checks out a similar book.

In any successful marketing campaign, the customer comes first. Library merchandising is no different. To increase circulation or to raise their profiles, libraries may not need continually to target nonusers. But libraries do need to place a new priority on effective service and on their current patrons' wants and needs. It might not mean providing drive-through service—although the Allentown Public Library in Pennsylvania does—but it does mean listening to users. When asked about his library's impressive circulation statistics, Greg Buss of the Richmond Public Library in British Columbia said the library simply takes patron comments very seriously. "Customers have never been shy about what they want," he explained, "but I think we have been shy in giving it to them."[36] Recovering from that shyness means adopting more customer-friendly policies. Standardizing circulation periods, for example, could eliminate confusion and encourage patrons to take out more books, just as take-no-prisoners overdue policies often reduce turnover. Giving patrons what they want also means having a responsive staff that can talk about books and provide the best possible readers' advisory through conversation, lists, displays, and arrangement. Perhaps most of all, it means heeding Scilken's frequent reminder that our attempts to save time rarely result in the best service for the reader.[37] Effective in-house marketing and promotion stand not only to increase our circulation, but to improve our service.

Notes

In citing works in the notes, *U*L,* is used for a short title for the *U*N*A*B*A*S*H*E*D*[TM] Librarian: The "How I Run My Library Good" Letter[sm].

1. Marvin H. Scilken, "Getting New Adult Steady Users," *U*L,* no. 111 (1999): 29.
2. Joseph Deitch, "Portrait: Marvin Scilken," *Wilson Library Bulletin* 59, no. 3 (November 1984): 205–7; and Marvin H. Scilken, "Retrieving Overdues—Some Thoughts," *U*L* no. 107 (1998): 4–5.

3. Marvin H. Scilken, "Woo Non-Users as Supporters," *U*L* no. 100 (1996): 11–12.

4. Philip M. Clark, "Patterns of Consistent, Persistent Borrowing Behavior by High-Intensity Users of a Public Library," *Public Libraries* 37, no. 5 (September/October 1998): 304.

5. Marvin H. Scilken, "Shelving Genre Fiction," *U*L* no. 109 (1998): 9.

6. Jack Alan Hicks, "Cappuccino Bars and Fragrance Gardens (Megabookstores and Public Libraries)," *U*L* no. 92 (1994): 21–22.

7. Marvin H. Scilken, "Classify to 'Merchandise,'" *U*L* no. 92 (1994): 23.

8. Sharon L. Baker and F. Wilfrid Lancaster, *The Measurement and Evaluation of Library Services* 2d ed. (Arlington, Va.: Information Resources Press, 1991), 27.

9. Sharon L. Baker, "Will Fiction Classification Schemes Increase Use?" *RQ* 27, no. 3 (Spring 1988): 366–76.

10. Amanda McGrady, "Putting Fiction Back Together," *U*L* no. 76 (1990): 6.

11. Jeffrey Cannell and Eileen McClusky, "Genrefication: Fiction Classification and Increased Circulation," in *Guiding the Reader to the Next Book*, ed. Kenneth D. Shearer (New York: Neal-Schuman Publishers, 1996), 159–65.

12. Scilken, "Shelving Genre Fiction," 9.

13. Baker, "Will Fiction Classification Schemes Increase Use?" 375.

14. Scilken, "Shelving Genre Fiction," 9.

15. Hicks, "Cappucino Bars," 21.

16. Merle Jacob, "Weeding the Fiction Collection Or Should I Dump *Peyton Place*?" *Reference & User Services Quarterly* 40, no. 3 (Spring 2001): 234–39.

17. Scilken, "Shelving Genre Fiction," 9.

18. Sharon L. Baker, "A Decade's Worth of Research on Browsing Fiction Collections," in *Guiding the Reader to the Next Book* ed. Kenneth D. Shearer (New York: Neal-Schuman Publishers, 1996), 127.

19. Baker, "A Decade's Worth," 127–47.

20. Chris Rippel, "Booklists Help Browsers Select Books," *U*L* no. 107 (1998): 5

21. Marian S. Edsall, *Library Promotion Handbook* (Phoenix: Oryx Press, 1980).

22. Edsall, *Library Promotion Handbook.*

23. Joyce G. Saricks and Nancy Brown, *Readers' Advisory Service in the Public Library* 2d ed. (Chicago: American Library Association, 1997).

24. Que Bronson, *Books on Display* (Washington, D.C.: Metropolitan Washington Library Council, 1982).

25. Baker, "A Decade's Worth," 140.

26. Scilken, "Shelving Genre Fiction," 9.

27. Robert Smith, "You Too Can Increase Your Circulation! (or My Circulation is Up)," *U*L* no. 111 (1999): 28–29.

28. Smith, "You Too Can Increase," 28–29.

29. Smith, "You Too Can Increase," 28–29.

30. Peter Eager, "Do You Want Fries with That? (Use Marketing Questions to Promote Library Materials and Services)" *U*L* no. 92 (1991): 11.

31. "Bestseller Club," *U*L* no. 105 (1995): 13.

32. Martha Vreeland, "Hot Titles," *U*L* no. 100 (1996): 12.

33. Mimi Morris, "Books You Might Have Missed," *U*L* no. 111 (1999): 29.

34. Rippel, "Booklists," 5.

35. Rippel, "Booklists," 5.

36. Evan St. Lifer, "Tapping into the Zen of Marketing," *Library Journal* 126, no. 8 (May 1, 2001): 44–47.

37. Scilken, Shelving Genre Fiction," 9.

Chapter 3

Selection with Scilken

Regan Robinson

"What I'm talking about is service to out of school adult users. That's my focus, that's what I am interested in, and everything I say will be related to that." With that disclaimer, Marvin Scilken, retired public library director and publisher for over twenty years of the *U*N*A*B*A*S*H*E*D Librarian*, sails into an explanation of how public librarians can (or should) select books.[1]

Book selection, he says, (he shuns terms like collection development or collection management), is time-consuming, "not hard," but time consuming and "a lot of bother." Retired now from the position he held for thirty years as director of the Orange (New Jersey) Public Library, Mr. Scilken admits to missing the "fun and bother" of buying books.

Readers familiar with his popular newsletter know that Mr. Scilken writes about library work with passion, directness, and missionary fervor. His comments that open each newsletter are short and challenging. He is also a frequent letter writer to *Library Journal*, the *New York Times* (his hometown newspaper), and any other publication that engages him.

"The fact that bookstores and the Book of the Month Club are in business, I consider a failure to the library operation. If we were really good, we would have their customers." After a pause, he adds, "I guess that's too much to ask for."

"A popular book will circulate many more times than an unpopular book. If you are interested in cost per circulation, the best buy is a book that is going to go out a lot."

The library has to have the books readers want, a seemingly simple concept. "It was the same in Ben Franklin's day. He started a library because people wanted to read more books than they cared to buy or to dust."

Book selection "isn't a desk job, although you have to spend some time with book review media."

Read What They Read

Read the reviewing media that your public reads, Mr. Scilken admonishes. "Your public doesn't read *Publishers Weekly* (*PW*), they certainly don't read *Library Journal*." He does read *PW* explaining that he reads the "Forecasts" from the bottom up—looking for the information on press run and advertising budget.

He relies on the *New York Times Book Review, Newsweek, Time*—"all those sources that your readers are reading."

Mr. Scilken details his own set of instructions for using the *New York Times Book Review*. "I have found an inverse relation between the length of review and popularity of the book—generally speaking. The books with the very small reviews are the most popular." He warns particularly against books with a front-page review—"they are nonstarters, they go out infrequently if at all."

These cautions are given with part of his tongue tucked in his cheek, and he adds that this may be changing with the new editor.

Publishers help book selectors, Mr. Scilken maintains, by their ads. "Publishers don't usually advertise books that aren't selling. They believe in mercy death—books that aren't selling, aren't advertised."

Along with review media that library users read, Mr. Scilken also watches the book club selections and *Library Journal*'s (*LJ*) "PrePub Alert." *LJ*'s reviews are also useful for subjects not covered in the civilian media.

Talk to Them

"Readers should have a feeling that the library is interested in their reading and that they can depend on the library." As he said earlier, this isn't a desk job. "Selectors should be talking with library users. Find out what they are looking for, what they didn't find. Look to see what they are carrying out of the library." And then buy "similar books."

Selectors should regularly scan the book return trucks. At Orange Public Library staff stamped the date in the books when they were returned. This allowed staff to see quickly and at a glance the circulation activity. Automated circulation systems provide total circulation and may include date of last use. Mr. Scilken's system which was color coded by year, showed if the item had been sitting without any use for several years even if its last use was recent.

Market the Books

Mr. Scilken argues for maintaining the attractive physical appearance of books. "Change the plastic jackets if needed," he says. Rebinds are made more attractive by re-jacketing them with the dust jacket.

At Orange, the new book shelves featured a selection of about two thousand books. A book stayed on the new bookshelf as long as it had been borrowed within the past thirty days.

"Libraries lose a lot of circulation by not displaying new books." Mr. Scilken, now a library user rather than staffer, is frustrated by his local library's new book collection which isn't very new and also isn't in any kind of order.

The new book shelf is as great testing ground. If a book didn't circulate from there, it was a likely candidate for being withdrawn. He points out what many know to be true, but still difficult to act upon, that it costs money to hold on to a book so "it pays to get rid of the books that died right away." If a book doesn't find a reader on the new book shelf, it is unlikely to attract use once it joins the thousands on the regular shelves. "Public libraries are the kennels of the publishers' dogs," he says quoting himself.

The Place of Reserves

"Libraries should encourage reserves for books that they don't expect to get, the reserves will help the library to find holes in the collection." For bestsellers and popular titles, he argues that it is less expensive to purchase more copies and consequently deal with fewer reserves, reducing staff involvement and costs.

Once a reserve is placed, he urges staff to act quickly. Don't wait to find a review but use the publisher or author as criteria. "We looked at the publisher. If it is Random House or Simon & Schuster, why not buy it? Is the author familiar? If you spend time on the floor you know the borrower. A reader who reads popular books will select a popular book."

The public library he now uses won't accept a reserve until the title is listed in the book catalog—a process that takes several months. He finds it tedious and poor service to require the reader who has read a review or heard about a new book to hold onto the title information until its appearance in the book catalog.

Never Offend the Taxpayer

"Put this in italics: *thou shall not offend the taxpayer*. That means that one never shows a great number of copies of the same title on the shelf at one time." Don't leave yourself open to the charge of squandering taxpayer money just because for the moment the rush for a particular book has slowed. Mr. Scilken's rule of thumb was never to have more than two copies of any book in one place. "We would scatter the books, we might have six copies, but never in the same place." Some can go on book return carts or be included in displays and as soon as the shelf stock is gone, the books can be replaced.

Unabashed

The synonyms for unabashed include shameless, arrant, barefaced, blatant, brassy, brazen, impudent, and unblushing. Mr. Scilken revealed one other selection tip that may fit any of those terms.

We are all familiar with the reviews in the standard review media [that] most often conclude with the admonition—essential for public libraries. Like so many of us, Mr. Scilken knew "deep down in my heart that the book would never circulate." So back when the library had a card catalog he would purchase just the catalog cards from the vendor—not the book itself. The cards would be added to the catalog stamped with the phrase "The librarian would take pleasure in getting this book for you," instead of a location. "Just to see if anyone would ever ask for it." Few did. Selection

takes experience. Read as many magazines as your readers read. Talk to the readers. Find out what they are looking for, what they didn't find. Look to see what they are carrying. Look at what is being borrowed and then buy similar books. Act quickly. The most important time of a book's life is when it is new.

Notes

1. Regan Robinson, "Selection with Scilken," *Librarians Collection Letter: A Monthly Newsletter for Collection Development Staff* 5, no. 2 (July 1995): 1, 3, 6.

Chapter 4

ALA Council and the Ethos of Debate

Loriene Roy

I first met Marvin Scilken on a Saturday in February of 1997, the night before I was to join the ranks of the elite and seat myself with other members of Council, the policy-setting body of the American Library Association (ALA). Marvin and his gracious wife, Polly, treated me to dinner. It was a much more inviting option than the new Councilors' reception scheduled the same evening.

I had run for Council twice. The first time was by invitation of the ALA Council Nominating Committee in spring 1995. I had hoped one day to serve on Council, perhaps after a decade on various ALA Division committees, but the call from the Nominating Committee came earlier than I planned. I felt that refusing the nomination might close that door forever. I lost this first election, receiving nearly the fewest votes of any nominee for vacancies among the one hundred Councilors-at-Large. I learned at the following ALA Midwinter Meeting that the Diversity Council, a group of ALA members from traditionally underrepresented groups including the five ethnic organizations affiliated with ALA, had started a petition asking to have my name added to the ballot. The Social Responsibilities Round Table (SSRT) also supported my nomination and included my name on campaign literature they mass-mailed. The following June, I was elected by a bare margin and joined the last class of Councilors-at-Large to serve four-year terms.

Of course, I had long heard of Marvin, especially from my graduate students who, semester after semester, became enthralled with Marvin's peculiar and wonderful publication, the U*N*A*B*A*S*H*E*D Librarian (U*L). Typically, these were students in my "Public Libraries" class who tolerated the formalities of graduate school only because it was their ticket to their newfound profession. The U*L devotees were those interested in practical applications, eager to

27

test ideas, and confident of their quick advancement in library administration.

I expected Marvin to be a know-it-all, a library practitioner who would greet me by pooh-poohing library schools and questioning my competence to teach public librarians. Instead, he was gentle and polite, a true conversationalist, a listener as well as an opinionated talker. I met him with Polly Scilken at his side, offering her eternal smile, supporting Marvin. She and I shared a background in allied health. Polly was a nurse, and I had a short career as a medical radiologic technologist. As expected, we spoke about public libraries and about Council, but what I remember best is the comfortable conversation about travel, books, and family.

He left me with his business card. It was a busy advertisement for *U*L* complete with an image of the cover of a sample issue and excerpts of positive reviews from such publications as *Magazines for Libraries* and *Choice* and affirmations from librarians from New Mexico, Ohio, and California. This first offering began my collection of Marvin Scilken business cards, some of which he inscribed with suggestions of possible topics for manuscripts I should send him. I still have these cards in a box in my office. One asked me to write about how I was elected to Council. This chapter is my belated response to his request.

The Culture of ALA Council

When ALA's initial charter of 1879 was revised in 1942 it identified for the first time both the ALA Executive Board and a Council.[1] The basic duty of an ALA Councilor is to attend and participate at scheduled meetings, held at ALA Annual Conference and the ALA Midwinter Meeting. Between meetings Councilors receive notices via an electronic list, ALACOUN, one of over one hundred and fifty lists on the ALA server. ALACOUN provides important information, a discussion forum, and the acerbic communication of a minority of Councilors. Council also comes with a few perks. Councilors receive advance housing requests and white ribbons to affix to their conference badges. The Standing Council Orientation Committee also manages a suite at the conference headquarters hotel where Councilors may meet and relax.

Also, Councilors may be appointed to work between meetings on four types of Council committees: standing, two-year special, interdivisional, or joint. Councilors elected to the Committee on Committees help arrange committee appointments. In addition, Council or the ALA President can form various ad hoc committees. Eight Councilors are elected by Council to serve on the ALA Executive Board which also includes the current ALA Officers, Immediate Past-President, and Executive Director. During my term as a Councilor-at-Large I also served on the Committee on the Status of Women in Librarianship (COSWL), on the Nominating Committee, and on the Special Presidential Committee on Council Mentoring.

There are usually several social events scheduled for Councilors alone. These may include a Council orientation event, a dessert social, and the traditional Council breakfast hosted by the ALA President-Elect prior to Council III.

Chief among the elective meetings for Councilors is the Council Caucus. Caucuses are meetings for Council members to preview Council agendas and provide a platform for those who want to float an idea, air a complaint, or test a resolution.

The Organization of Council Meetings

Three Council meetings are scheduled over four days and total some ten hours of formal meeting time. These time slots, designated Council I, Council II, and Council III, each reflect a separate tradition in their agendas. Every Council opens with introductions and announcements from the Presiding Officer and then continues with the establishment of the quorum and Councilors standing at their selected places.

In accordance with ALA Policy, Council I is preceded by an ALA Council/Executive Board/Membership Information session.[2] There are reports from the ALA President, the Budget Analysis and Review Committee (BARC), the ALA Executive Director, the Endowment Trustees, and the President-Elect. ALA Presidential reports are accounts of progress on initiatives, tallies of air miles flown, and events attended to represent ALA interests. The agenda for Council I includes consent items, action items, information items, and new business. Consent items generally consist of approving previous Council minutes and announcing the appointment of tellers who will count ballots during that conference. Action items include the announcement of Councilors nominated to serve on the Council Committee on Committees and to the Planning and Budget Assembly. Information items consist of a report on the actions of the ALA Executive Board to implement motions and resolutions passed by Council and reports from ALA Divisions and from the Freedom to Read Foundation. Committee reports may include action items that require Council decisions. New resolutions appear under new business.

Honorary memberships are usually introduced at Council I. This is also when the Executive Board Candidates Forum is scheduled with each candidate presenting biographical information and responding to questions from the floor. The slate for the Executive Board has at least six names: those of six people nominated by the Council Committee on Committees and any other nominees from the floor. Councilors pick up ballots in the ALA Office or wait to vote until the ballot box is brought to Council II. The two candidates who receive the most votes are elected to the Executive Board.

The ALA Treasurer presents his or her report as an action report in Council II. This report is usually met with a call for more explanatory tables. The rest of the agenda includes reports from task forces and committees and the introduction of resolutions. Another tradition during Council II is the acknowledgment of visiting dignitaries such as officers of organizations affiliated with ALA or officers of international organizations.

Tributes, memorials, and testimonials are read at Council III. Council III also sees the gavel handed over to the newly elected ALA President. The tellers report the number of votes each candidate to the Committee on Committees and to ALA Executive Board received. During the ALA Midwinter Meeting, Councilors take a break to view a video clip of the ALA President's appearance on NBC's "Today Show" congratulating the latest winners of the Caldecott and Newbery awards. These and other book awards are announced at a press conference on the Monday morning of ALA Midwinter. At the ALA Annual Conference retiring Councilors are noted and a group photograph is arranged during a scheduled break.

Difficult issues carry over as unfinished business from Council meeting to Council meeting, conference to conference. Recently, there have been efforts to make Council meetings more efficient. The tentative agendas now list consent items that do not require debate and an estimated time allowance per agenda item. The Task Force on Council Formats surveyed Councilors in spring 1999. One hundred six of the 108 Councilors who responded advised following a consent agenda. All 108 wanted to receive more information in advance of meetings.[3]

Managing Life as an ALA Councilor: Seating and Records Management

My inaugural experience on the Council floor brought to mind the Spanish Inquisition. I had observed several Council meetings prior to my election but its rules and order were still not apparent to me. I arrived early to the assigned room, which was dark and cold and filled with long tables and chairs arranged at the foot of a dais. The dais is reserved for ALA royalty: the President, the President-Elect, the Executive Director, plus the Parliamentarian and one staff person. The Councilors' tables are marked with colored place settings which, upon closer examination, prove to be the day's "ALA Council Vote and Attendance Record" form. Scattered about the Council seating area are microphones, each bearing a numbered sign. ALA administrative staff is placed close to the dais while visitors sit outside the Council area.

Deciding where to sit turned out to be a challenging decision throughout my four-year term. I asked experienced councilors where to sit. One responded that she chose a spot near where the late Elizabeth Futas would sit. I learned quickly that there was a designated area for the rabble-rousers—representatives from the Social Responsibilities Round Table and some members of the ethnic organizations affiliated with ALA. These folks can be counted on to vote against a motion to close debate no matter how long a topic has been discussed. Their station was the last few rows of the seating section facing the dais and close to the library press in the audience. Late night party-goers, some sporting sunglasses, decamped mid-rows in the section to the left of the dais.

I tested the waters, sitting front and center and both left and right of the dais. I deigned seats unacceptable if they were too close to Councilors who chattered throughout the proceedings. Once I seated myself next to another Councilor from Texas, only to discover that our voting records were diametrically opposite. She was a dazzler, high-heeled and swathed in mink. We bobbed up and down, taking turns rising to signal our voting decision. Finally, it was all too apparent that she glared at me each time our votes diverged. This wasn't my seat, either. By the end of my term, I had found my home: mid-row to the right of the dais with my back to the exit. This location afforded me easy access to the restroom, a quick escape to the exhibits, and a good view of the projection screens that displayed the simultaneous captioning of Council proceedings.

In addition to seat selection, Councilors are concerned with records management. It takes an inordinate amount of time to sort out the myriad Council documents. This involves winding through the pick-up station, a long table on which the day's numbered, color coded documents are displayed. The station is a prime socializing area for many Councilors who greet each other like long-lost screen stars bussing cheeks and occasionally emitting high-pitched squeals. It is, after all, a sorority. The stack of papers near any one Councilor's table can become impressive. I usually added a small reference collection: the most recent *ALA Handbook of Organization* and a copy of the accepted parliamentary procedure rules, Sturgis.[4,5]

ALA Councilors and the Ethos of Debate

Councilors interpret their roles in several ways. The great majority are silent voters, who stand or stay seated to register their opinion. They dutifully sign and log their votes on the day's color voting form and submit it to tellers at the end of Council. *American Libraries* publishes the voting records of each Councilor. A small number of Councilors can be expected to speak at each meeting, introducing new motions or entering in debate. Following proper Council etiquette, they register their intent to talk by standing in front of a numbered microphone and, when called on by the Chair, introduce themselves by name and rank—as Councilor-at-Large, Chapter Councilor, Division Councilor, or Round Table Councilor.

Marvin was a frequent speaker at Council sessions, a familiar figure standing patiently for the presiding officer to call his microphone number. I recall that he often held some piece of paper in hand, adding to his resemblance to a burly Spencer Tracey news reporter. He was an unabashed Councilor and his reputation led to his five-time election to Council. Other Councilors, impatient to make progress through the agenda items, might have tired of Marvin's frequent contributions. But just when you least expected it, Marvin would help clarify an issue, state what many had been thinking but had been leery of expressing, or insert a charming turn of phrase that added a well-needed bit of levity to some grave debate. Marvin and Herb Biblo, another long-standing Councilor, would take turns at the microphone like dueling New York Public Library lions. They were champions of the ethos of debate.

I recall one lengthy discussion about electronic communication and the possibility of virtual participation on Council. Marvin was held up as the example of the exclusionary nature of electronic participation. He had been the sole Councilor not to have e-mail access. He strode to a microphone to set the record straight: he now could read e-mail but he implored his colleagues not to send him any.

Marvin told me that I had an obligation to speak up at Council. I took his advice and found the opportunity to speak at the microphone at each Council meeting I attended.

My first comment, at Council I, on a Sunday in February 1997 was to register my opposition to charging for exhibits-only badges. I spent my first five years as an ALA conference attendee dedicated to exploring the exhibits. My argument against charging was that students in schools of library and information science were being priced out of attending ALA conferences. Free exhibit passes were one way to entice future professionals to attend and perhaps to become actively involved in ALA.

Now, I knew that my argument made sense to me, but I am sure that no one at Council that day understood a word. The one thing I did right was to keep my comments within the three minute limit for debate. I do recall that I directed my comments to Elizabeth Martinez, ALA Executive Director, and found warmth and concern. I sat down quickly and was sure that I had made a fool of myself, but Polly Scilken gave me a thumbs-up from the audience. I was hooked on making her and Marvin proud of me. My subsequent trips to the microphone never improved. I was plagued by "Elvis leg syndrome" as I held one leg rigid while the other sought to escape. Hands sweating, my voice erupted in a key higher than normal speech, at five times normal speed.

The drafting and introducing resolutions can also be a fearsome prospect. Guidelines for preparing resolutions are printed in the ALA Policy Manual, in each Conference program, in distribution bins, and also as a Council document.[6] Resolutions may be drafted before conference on the Council electronic list or at on site. Councilors can also seek advice from the ALA Parliamentarian as well as from experienced Councilors.

A Councilor may draft a resolution in response to his or her concern about a specific issue. Interested ALA personal members or ALA units may approach a Councilor with an idea or draft for a resolution. Resolutions should state clearly the rationale for the resolution and need to be framed in one or more "whereas" clauses. Resolutions need to be moved by one Councilor and seconded by another, both of whom sign the bottom of resolution. Resolutions may also list the various committees, round tables, or divisions that support it. One signer then brings the resolution draft before the Council Resolutions Committee at least twenty-four hours before it is presented to Council. These Committee members staff a table in the ALA office in the convention center. Once approved and initialed by the Resolutions Committee, it is stamped and numbered then duplicated to appear in the line of documents to be picked up from the distribution table at the next Council meeting.

The resolution initiators then enter the political process of garnering support for the resolution. This may entail reminding Councilors that a given resolution is scheduled for a particular Council meeting. It may also mean recruiting Councilors to contribute comments endorsing an issue on the floor of Council. At Council, those who present the resolution must provide the Secretariat with copies to project on the screens, read the resolution following the "therefore be it resolved" clauses, and must respond to questions that arise from the floor.

Beyond drafting and presenting resolutions, Councilors engage in discussion on the Council floor, all guided by the accepted parliamentary procedure. In addition to the main motion, Councilors may apply subsidiary motions. An example of a subsidiary motion is a motion to refer a resolution with potential fiscal implications to Budget Analysis and Review Committee for review. This motion usually includes a request that BARC report back before the end of the conference. There are also privileged motions, such as the move to recess, and incidental motions, such as calling for a point of order. There are rules governing which changes may be made to main motions, such as motions to reconsider or rescind. Thus Council action is more complex than presenting of a resolution or calling the vote or question. I learned quickly that Councilors with a command of Sturgis were in a more favorable position, though the Parliamentarian assured me that even these Councilors were often wrong in their interpretations.

ALA members can overturn a Council decision with a quorum of one percent of the total membership at an ALA Membership Meeting. Since only two official meetings have been held since 1994, the chances of ALA membership overriding a Council vote are small.[7]

At my last turn at the microphone in Chicago in July 2000 I presented a resolution to establish a new Council committee on literacy. I overhead that a Councilor asked why I always presented resolutions for people who asked me at the last minute. Granted, it sometimes meant that I appeared unprepared, but I was honored to be asked and those who asked me knew even less about the operations of Council than I did. Later that day, this Councilor also questioned my vote against a motion he thought I would favor. "I can't believe you didn't vote for this," he called out to me on the Council floor. Perhaps becoming notorious, at least to one other Councilor, was a measure of my arrival as a Councilor. Incidentally, the resolution on the literacy committee was passed by acclamation and a round of applause. The secret was good timing. This resolution was the last to be heard at Council III and followed an hour-long acrimonious discussion on outsourcing, a continually divisive topic. Councilors wanted to leave conference with at least an agreement on a topic that they all supported, literacy.

Serving on Council is an economic investment. It requires Councilors to arrive on Saturday evening at the latest and stay through the conference to the very end, a full day after the exhibits area closes, after the ALA Presidential Inaugural Banquet, and after the closing of the Internet cafe. The expenses of serving on Council make it difficult for some ALA members to participate in the democratic process.

What Really Matters

My last image of Marvin on the Council floor was him sitting in the peanut gallery during a break, his arm around a smiling Polly. I saw him later that afternoon at the ALA Council Caucus where he asked, as he had done before, why ALA Midwinter was frequently scheduled in one of the coldest areas of the country while ALA Annual was scheduled in torridly hot locales. Still, he said he would tolerate this absurdity, promising to see all of us in New Orleans the following summer, simply because he liked us. I saw Marvin briefly at the Council reception held later that evening in an open-reception area in a conference hotel. I recall that it was crowded and that there weren't enough chairs to relax in. I remember that Marvin looked tired and, perhaps, a little cranky.

I rushed to Council the next morning, worried as usual about the upcoming battle and the lengthy agenda. I expected a routine Council III with its ranks of Councilors slowly depleting around noon, as people departed for flights that would take them home. This would be followed by a call for a quorum count and then the closing of the meeting when attendance dipped below seventy-five Councilors. I recall that someone stopped me as I was about to enter the Council room, just as someone stopped each Councilor that morning. He told me that Marvin had passed away just a few hours before. All of a sudden, the agenda was not so lengthy and the impending arguments were not so monumental. We assembled, and ALA President Ann Symons opened the meeting with tears and a more formal announcement of Marvin's death. At the center of the room lay a table with a memorial book, pen on a table, and a small bouquet of flowers. Surprisingly and lovingly, Polly Scilken sat in the audience to witness the gathering of friends. Many Councilors spoke, including many of the newer Councilors who described how Marvin had mentored them, as he had mentored me. This was one time when I did not go to the microphone. I knew I could not speak without crying, though these tears did come anyway when Mitch Freedman honored Marvin by singing, "Young at Heart."

To Serve Again on Council?

My initial response to the end of my term was relief. I longed to devote my attention to action research and working in a more collaborative setting, possibly on some small ALA Division committees. Still I valued my time on Council. I appreciated the intense learning opportunity. I valued witnessing library history in the making, especially the lengthy discussions. I saw the passage of ALA's Policy on Filtering.[8] I saw the change in term lengths in 1998 and the addition of Councilors elected by Round Tables. Now, the five Round Tables with the greatest number of members can each elect a Councilor. The remaining Round Tables elect a Councilor to represent them all.

Serving on Council helped me bring content to my graduate classes. I witnessed controversy. During the debate on the Boy Scouts of America issue, I watched two middle-aged male Councilors approach the microphones in their beige, festooned Boy Scout uniforms. I observed Sandy Berman's call for ALA to support him in a complaint against his employer. I learned more about the structure and operation of ALA, and I came to value the quiet competence of many ALA staff members. I always felt like an outsider, but I learned to adapt to the culture of Council. I chuckled with others at the misspellings projected on the screens. I acted like I knew what I was doing. Some ALA members still approach me at Conference, rough resolutions in hand, asking me to help get their request before Council. I added to my skills and challenged my natural inclination toward shyness. And I made friends, including Marvin Scilken.

I still return to Council to sit in the peanut gallery, this time to enjoy the show. It doesn't look too frightening from the outside. Sometimes I still join the line of Councilors to pick up a copy of the printed agenda. I am a read-only subscriber to ALACOUN where I continue to monitor Councilor's discussions and communication to Council from ALA.

Would I have done things differently? I would have prepared more. I would have spent more time with Sturgis, acquiring the mighty power of parliamentary procedure. And I would have tried to speak more at the microphone. Would I do it again if the Nominations Committee called or someone circulated another petition? Yes.

Notes

1. "Charter of 1979 (revised 1942)," *ALA Handbook of Organization 2001-2002* (Chicago: American Library Association, 2001), 8.
2. "ALA Policy Manual, Section One, Organization and Operational Policies, Policy 5.5.2, Council/Executive Board/Membership Session," *ALA Handbook of Organization 2001-2002* (Chicago: American Library Association, 2001), 32.
3. Julie G. Huiskamp, "Results of Evaluation of Council Agenda and Format Changes." Online posting. ALACOUN discussion list. Available E-mail: alacoun@ala1.ala.org. 11 July 1999.
4. *ALA Handbook of Organization 2001-2002* (Chicago: American Library Association, 2001).
5. Alice Sturgis, *The Standard Code of Parliamentary Procedure.* 3rd ed new and rev. (New York: McGraw-Hill, 1988).
6. "ALA Policy Manual, Section One, Organization and Operational Policies, Policy 5.3, Council Resolutions: Guidelines for Preparation of Resolutions to Council," *ALA Handbook of Organization 2001-2002* (Chicago: American Library Association, 2001), 32.
7. Larry Romans, "Membership Meeting Quorum." Online posting. ALACOUN discussion list. Available E-mail: alacoun@ala1.ala.org. 3 January 2002.
8. "ALA Policy Manual, Section Two, Positions and Public Policy Statements, Policy 53.1.16," *ALA Handbook of Organization 2001-2002* (Chicago: American Library Association, 2001), 46.

Chapter 5

Cataloging: The First Public Service

Joanna F. Fountain

A person walks in the door of a library and expects to find a collection of books and other materials, a librarian *or at least a catalog*, and maybe a table and chairs. In the absence of an accurate, current catalog, the librarian is expected to fill the role of guide to the collection. The librarian, on the other hand, cannot be expected to have total recall and expects to be assisted by the cataloger in the process of guiding the user through the maze of information and ideas found in each individual library.

It is a privilege to act as a guide, either directly in reference services, or indirectly through catalog services. As librarians in either role, we are entrusted with the responsibility and joy of leading individuals of all stripes toward their next encounter in the world of the mind. People share with us clues to their desired or intended direction, sometimes very private details, in the hopes that we will fulfill their needs. Then we must use every tool at our disposal to make the journey as short, quick, and accurate as possible, sometimes using a series of clues discovered and surrendered only as we move closer or farther from the person's real or actual goals.

The library's catalog contains many of these clues. Bibliographic records, acting as surrogates in the catalog for items both in the library's collection and remotely accessible, are essentially patterned sets of clues to the content and form of information contained in the items themselves. A book's title is one clue to its content. Subject headings provide others. Notes add more detail and depth, and so on through each element provided. The more clues and the more accurate and comprehensible the clues are, the better each record is able to perform its functions of finding and helping to interpret the work it represents, allowing the work to be collocated physically or virtually with similar materials.

Wonderfully helpful records are combinations of straightforward and interpretive data; one or more forms of a work's title, and the names of its creators are essential. A single title taken from a pre-designated chief source of information may or may not be enough to accomplish the task of communicating the functional title of the work. So variant forms of the title that appear (or could appear) in other locations or in spoken usage are invaluable additions. A person's name—an author, illustrator, compiler, etc.—will often appear in more than one form, and each such form must be accounted for after designating the most frequently used form as its "authorized" form. Finally, the notes that explain and interpret elements that are not clear from other parts of the description may be vital clues that allow the seeker to move forward, alternately reinforcing and/or changing the direction of the search.

By providing just these three elements, the cataloger would have taken a significant step toward accomplishing the goals of the searcher. The catalog would have provided access to an item by its title and "author," and some basic interpretive information would be available to evaluate the work's usefulness for a given person's particular needs. But a good catalog does much more; it also gives some idea of the subject and form of the content, provides information and access points for use in collocating materials, and gives verbal direction to information about the work beyond that contained in the title or notes.

Charles Cutter suggested three basic objectives for a useful catalog, each in turn requiring that the catalog always yield information by "author, title, and subject."[1] The first objective is *to identify and find* known items. The second objective is designed to help the searcher *to discover* additional related works through connective headings and other wording, and the third enables seekers *to choose* among works and items for the desired purpose prior to having them in hand. The best cataloging records provide for each objective through the use of multiple, generous access points for all persons with creative or intellectual responsibility, all appropriate variations of titles, and a variety of helpful subject entries.

Where and How Does This Fit with Marvin Scilken's Views?

First and foremost, Scilken believed that the object of cataloging changes "*should be simplification, not the erection of more barriers to effective catalog-utilization.*"[2]

He recommended creating simple records, eliminating unrecognizable elements (such as control numbers) from the public view of a record. On the other hand, he advocated including numbers that facilitate retrieval, such as LCCNs (Library of Congress card/control numbers).[3]

He insisted that changes to the catalog, especially in terms of location and status of materials, should be kept current to minimize confusion on the part of users.[4]

He advocated what he called "a people's approach to cataloging."[5]

He expressed his agreement with Sanford (Sandy) Berman at the ALA Conference in Las Vegas (1973) that it is not helpful to use abbreviations and special, denotative punctuation "plus ISBD data," and hoped that "one day *all* words would be spelled out on catalog-copy to minimize frustration and misunderstanding."[6]

In the interest of timeliness, he recommended automating as many processes as possible, but using manual methods when those are faster.[7] Later he reminded readers that "studies have shown [that] people are looking for newer material, and because of technical and cost considerations the very newest materials [should] appear in . . . catalogs."[8]

His answer to dilemmas of lack of access to reserve materials was to purchase more materials to satisfy such requests.[9]

Scilken thought ISBD(M) (International Standard Bibliographic Description—Monographs) would "turn off" the user. He believed that it made cataloging data more mystifying rather than simpler.[10] Those and other standards have since been modified more than once but still do not meet Scilken's standard for understandability.

He did not believe that libraries should follow so willingly the "siren song" of LC records when they don't solve the user's "finding-problems."[11] In explaining his disapproval of ISBD(M), he states that "Our gains seem to be at the cost of catalog intelligibility," recommending that we "catalog public library books for public library users and potential users" and "make our catalogs 'people-readable.'"[12] He further suggested dropping or suppressing most elements of "description" except publication date, favoring subject access to library materials instead, except in the shelf list. He cites Harry Dewey's "law" that what saves the librarian's time usually costs the reader his/hers.[13] This view does crop up among librarians now and then, and the creating of "core-level" record seems to try to address aspects of this situation; however, there seems to be little support for it at this time, especially among academic-library catalogers who indeed write many of the original records found on the Internet.

Regarding subject entries, he was "a believer in specific entry," preferring direct entry over inverted entries, such as "Mass merchandising," "Letter carriers" and "Candlemaking." He hoped for a revision of other entries, such as "Best books" instead of such pre-coordinated combinations as "Bibliography—Best Books." He advocated, wherever possible, terminology "used by real people," such as "Middle ages." He also preferred deletion of most "U.S." and "United States" headings and subdivisions in most subject and author entries.[14]

He strongly supported the idea of assigning subject headings to works of fiction when one or more definite topics can be discerned.[15] The publication of not one, but two editions of *Guidelines on Subject Access to Individual Works of Fiction, Drama, Etc.* is evidence of the popularity of this idea among librarians in all types of libraries—not just public libraries where the need has always been most evident.[16]

He also believed in creating subject headings for fictional characters (such as "Inspector Maigret") and adding these to catalogs with the "—Fiction" subdivision to enhance findability, taking into account the manner in which many readers identify relevant Simenon novels in a library's collection.[17]

Scilken also advocated the addition of more title entries, not only as analytics, but also for variant titles, such as "added entries for subtitles, catchwords, permuted titles, cover titles, and jacket titles."[18] He mentioned these again later, stating that one should "routinely add key words, partial titles, synthetic titles, misspellings, etc."[19] He would undoubtedly be pleased to see the implementation by catalogers of ever more MARC "246" entries in cataloging records for just this sort of title access.

There is not much evidence of whether his ideas on introducing "public" or "scope" notes referring to vertical-file material have been implemented, as these tend to be viewable only within local catalogs.[20] While it is relatively simple in the online environment to create such notes, Hennepin County Library's catalog has included notes of this type since 1974.

Another suggestion he made that may not yet be widely implemented, but which would be very helpful to catalog-users, is the addition of alternative spellings and forms of names *not* found on materials but which are likely to be used by searchers.[21] The Library of Congress, which maintains the international name-authority files, provides for no such alternative forms of access in name-authority records, which is to the detriment of users' retrieval attempts. Some automation-system vendors have tried to overcome this difficulty by providing background word-equivalency tables, including both misspellings and alternative English-language spellings. It is an excellent beginning, but catalogers should be alert to possible additions in the reference structure of local catalogs, enhancing the value of the catalog at any opportunity beyond the automatic capabilities of their systems. It is the kind of "value-added" work that can gain catalogers appreciation beyond that gained by less obvious aspects of currency and accuracy in records.

As Maurice J. Freedman said, "Marvin Scilken is one of the few people who can look at technical services wholly unburdened by 'the past,' the 'we've always done it this way' fixation, etc., ad nauseam. We are grateful to him for the fresh ideas and approaches he shared with us, some of which have already been implemented."[22]

Considering classification and call numbers, Scilken advocated using "old numbers for old subjects and new numbers for new subjects," a scheme that Michael Gorman suggests would be "subject to little or no change."[23] Because call numbers are so local in their application, it is difficult to determine to what extent this approach to classification changes may have been implemented in American or other libraries.

On the other hand, Scilken's idea of a good public view matches many current computer displays, which label the elements in the ISBD record in a transparent way, eliminating much of the "translation" that users must do when they read a record in its ISBD/AACR2 form—with punctuation providing the only clues to interpreting the record.[24] Among his examples:

Author: Norris, Gunilla B.
  Title: The good morrow; drawings by Charles Robinson.
  Publisher: Atheneum. Year of publication: 1969.
  92 pages

vs. Norris, Gunilla Brodde, 1939-
       The good morrow / Gunilla B. Norris ; drawings
by Charles Robinson. – 1st ed. — New York : Atheneum
Publishers, 1969.
       92 p. : ill. ; 21 cm.[25]

No matter how technical one has to be to create it, the purpose of a library catalog is service. And it is the first service people expect when they walk into any library. A catalog is what distinguishes a library from any other accumulation of books and other materials. Until such a collection has been cataloged, is not really accessible to a new user—a new public needing guidance to the information and ideas it contains.

NOTES

    1.   Cutter, Charles A. *Rules for a Dictionary Catalog, 4th ed.* (Washington, D.C.: U.S. Government Printing Office, 1904): 11–12.
    2.   Hennepin County Library. Cataloging Section. *Cataloging Bulletin* no. 2 (July 13, 1973): 4.
    3.   Hennepin County Library. Cataloging Section. *Cataloging Bulletin* no. 4 (Nov. 21, 1973): 7–8.
    4.   Hennepin County Library. Cataloging Section. *Cataloging Bulletin* no. 4 (Nov. 21, 1973): 6–7.
    5.   Hennepin County Library. Cataloging Section. "Cataloging: State of the Art," *Cataloging Bulletin* no. 4 (Nov. 21. 1973): 25.
    6.   Hennepin County Library. Cataloging Section. *Cataloging Bulletin* no. 2 (July 13, 1973): 3–4.
    7.   Hennepin County Library. Cataloging Section. "Small is Beautiful," *Cataloging Bulletin* no. 4 (Nov. 21, 1973): 7.
    8.   Hennepin County Library. Cataloging Section. *Cataloging Bulletin* no. 34 (May/June 1978): 23.
    9.   Hennepin County Library. Cataloging Section. *Cataloging Bulletin* no. 4 (Nov. 21, 1973): 7.
    10.   Hennepin County Library. Cataloging Section. *Cataloging Bulletin* no. 4 (Nov. 21, 1973): 9.
    11.   Hennepin County Library. Cataloging Section. *Cataloging Bulletin* no. 4 (Nov. 21, 1973): 9.
    12.   Hennepin County Library. Cataloging Section. *Cataloging Bulletin* no. 18/19 (Dec. 1, 1975): 3.
    13.   Hennepin County Library. Cataloging Section. *Cataloging Bulletin* no. 27 (April 1, 1977): 3.
    14.   Hennepin County Library. Cataloging Section. *Cataloging Bulletin* no. 4 (Nov. 21, 1973) : 2–3.
    15.   Hennepin County Library. Cataloging Section. *Cataloging Bulletin* no. 5 (Jan. 21, 1974): 5.
    16.   American Library Association. Association for Library Collections and Technical Services. Subject Analysis Committee. *Guidelines on Subject Access to Individual Works of Fiction, Drama, etc.* Chicago: American Library Association, 1990.

17. Hennepin County Library. Cataloging Section. *Cataloging Bulletin* no. 5 (Jan. 21, 1974): 5.

18. Hennepin County Library. Cataloging Section. *Cataloging Bulletin* no. 5 (Jan. 21, 1974): 5.

19. Hennepin County Library. Cataloging Section. "Small is Beautiful," *Cataloging Bulletin* no. 34 (May/June 1978): 23.

20. Hennepin County Library. Cataloging Section. *Cataloging Bulletin* no. 5 (Jan. 21, 1974): 5.

21. Hennepin County Library. Cataloging Section. *Cataloging Bulletin* no. 5 (Jan. 21, 1974): 5.

22. Hennepin County Library. Cataloging Section. *Cataloging Bulletin* no. 4 (Nov. 21, 1973): 10.

23. Gorman, Michael. "The Longer the Number, the Smaller the Spine; or, Up and Down with Melvil and Elsie." *American Libraries* 12 no. 8 (Sept. 1981): 498–499 .

24. Hennepin County Library. Cataloging Section. *Cataloging Bulletin* no. 27 (Apr. 1, 1977): 3.

25. Hennepin County Library. Cataloging Section. *Cataloging Bulletin* no. 27 (Apr. 1, 1977): 3.

Part II

In His Own Words

Chapter 6

A Conversation with Marvin H. Scilken

Joseph Deitch

In 1992, I spent a day with Marvin H. Scilken, director of the Orange (New Jersey) Public Library. Scilken was widely known as a library crusader and as the most eminent debunker of things librarians hold sacred. He passionately espoused libraries as centers for books and reading. Anyone who called libraries "the infrastructure of the mind," as Scilken did, is worth listening to and reading about.

Scilken's Management Philosophy

A day spent following Scilken on the job offered more practical knowledge than a year at many a good library school. He could, at the drop of a book, reel off more good practices for better library management than any top executive at the American Library Association (ALA).

Scilken took me on a tour of the library. With its Greek revival exterior and Renaissance interior, the library building had been given landmark status eleven years prior to our meeting. "We also give landmark library service," Scilken noted.

> The ways of doing things from one generation to another without change ought to be challenged. What if doctors, surgeons, and scientists locked themselves into one system, into concrete. That's the trouble with libraries: they exist and function by the status quo. They don't want to change. The library field, like all professional fields, needs a good shaking up once in a while.

Scilken described his own approach for managing a public library:

> All directors have a different style. My style is to be involved personally in all
> library activities. I enjoy solving problems. I enjoy talking to people. I like to
> talk about libraries. I speak to readers every day. I'm out on the floor, and I talk
> to people and keep honing operations with user input. I enjoy the work. I think
> we are on the cutting edge of good library management. It is all driven by our
> trying to be as imaginative as possible to meet the needs of our clients. Our
> entire operation here is customer-based.
>
> A good library is dependent on a good library staff. There is no one way of
> managing a library. What may be good management in this library may not be
> elsewhere. You and I were cheap, relatively speaking. Now people are
> expensive. Seventy to 80 percent of our budget goes for people and a small
> amount for books. In today's library, you want a good staff and a happy staff. A
> library is as good as its staff, regardless of its holdings.

A Brief Biography

In addition to introducing his professional philosophy and achievements, Scilken
reflected on his career and personal history:

> Coming to Orange was a big move for me. I remember standing across from the
> library and looking at it in 1962 or 1963 and thinking how wonderful it would be
> to be the librarian in that library. I've been here nearly thirty years and it has
> been a lot of fun.
>
> As a boy I regularly visited the Fordham Library Center Branch of the New
> York Public Library. It was nearest to my home. I had to walk, and it was quite a
> distance, maybe a couple of miles. I loved it, and I love libraries. I was not very
> good at sports. I think that those not good at sports tend to go to reading. I also
> bought a lot of books, and my mother bought books for me. My parents didn't
> read books. My sister did.
>
> I came late to libraries. I became a librarian in the early 1960s. I had
> worked for my dad, who was in the refrigeration and commercial furnace
> business. I was very unhappy doing that kind of work. Then I answered an ad in
> the *New York Times*. It said: 'Become a librarian. Wire Albany.' So I wired
> Albany, and they admitted me to a test. I came out high on it. I got a tuition
> scholarship and applied to the Columbia University library school. The school
> asked for an essay on my life and why I wanted to be a librarian. I dawdled so
> much that time ran out and I failed to get in. I asked if there was another library
> school in the area. He mentioned the Pratt Institute. I dashed down to Pratt and
> got admitted the same day. The rest is library history

He stopped frequently during our tour to discuss innovations and improvements
he introduced or planned to introduce. He reported on many of these practices in
the *U*N*A*B*A*S*H*E*D Librarian*, the tabloid-sized quarterly newsletter on
best library practices that he and his wife, Polly Scilken, edited and published. It
was obvious that Scilken's practice informed his writing. His experience on the
job contributed content to the *U*N*A*B*A*S*H*E*D Librarian* that he
described as "fresh, current, and relevant." His newspaper was, as he said, "full
of new ideas, methods, and slogans."

Scilken handed me a mock *Newsweek* special report on him. His image was reproduced on the cover with headlines reading, "Our Man of the Year," "The World Celebrates a Man for All Seasons," "Legend Tells His Story," and "How The Man Won, and Why." The last referred to his 1991 candidacy for President of ALA. Of four aspirants, Scilken came in last, but he had enough admirers nationwide to get on the ballot. "I still think the library profession badly needs my kind of leadership to help advance in professional respect and personnel benefits, including a sweeping national lift in salaries for librarians."

Scilken's campaign began when a friend called him and said that he should run:

He had called previously, years ago, and I figured that now I was getting on in years. If I ever was going to run for president, it would have to be this year. So I ran. I felt I had a different message from all the previous themes and messages that I had heard. It was that the ALA President can energize the association by coming up with one or two strong themes every year or so. My campaign idea was to sell libraries to the country through newspaper letter columns, to try to involve every member of the ALA to write to the local media, to flood the newspapers across the country with letters about libraries and to suggest articles about libraries to the press. I came out fourth in a field of four in the election. The ALA seems to favor women for the presidency. It's difficult for a man to get elected. I'm sixty-five, and I am thinking of retiring. I won't try again. If I came in second, I might have. But to come in last shows there is little interest in my candidacy. It didn't need an ALA presidential campaign to indicate that librarians don't like to write letters about libraries.

Certainly the highlight of my career was when I blew the whistle on the publishers' pricing system and brought it to the attention of the Senate Antitrust and Monopoly Subcommittee. In 1966 I testified before the subcommittee in Washington and told them that the publishers were overcharging libraries. They had one price for all books going to libraries, whether a library bought ten thousand books or one book. They charged high prices. They stole $54 million worth of books by price fixing. It wasn't just price fixing but price gouging. It was enormously profitable for the publishers whose tactics I exposed and attacked in Washington. I sued them all in what was, I think, one of the bravest acts in library history. What they were doing was against the law. The publishers made no secret of it. They even advertised this practice. Librarians wrote to the American Book Publisher's Association, saying, 'You're screwing us and we want you to stop it.' I wrote a lot of letters to the Federal Trade Commission, to senators, and to others about that publishing situation, but they ignored me. The only people who paid attention were Senators Clifford Case and Philip A. Hart. Senator Case and his associates pursued the matter and got indictments of individual publishers. Later, I found out that the antitrust lawyer in Chicago discovered these unfair pricing and monopoly tactics. When the hearings were called, he got permission to sue the publishers under the Sherman Antitrust Act. All the publishers except Doubleday and Little Brown were indicted for civil and criminal acts. They pleaded no contest and were fined $250,000. School boards and library boards started a thousand separate civil suits against the publishers were started all over the country. The school and library boards collected $10 million and the lawyers got $8 million.

I have mixed feelings about publishers. Every time publishers discover libraries, we get screwed. They overcharge and screw us. They view libraries as a market easy to squeeze and deceive. We get short discounts and high prices so

the publishers who sell primarily to libraries do very well indeed. They have
been very poor in pushing reading. As far as I know, they give no money to
National Library Week. So I think that if they just publish good books and bring
people into bookstores, maybe that's the best they can do.

Scilken's efforts were widely recognized. Although he noted:

I never got a letter of thanks from anybody in the U.S. library system, I mean,
officially. I got letters from my colleagues, but the library associations at that
time, or since, have never done anything about what I believe was an historic
service to American libraries. The hearings got no coverage. They ignored it. It
was never reported in the media, including the major newspapers and journals,
yet it was a book event of historic significance. Many years later, the *New York
Times* ran a small story on the settlement of one of those suits.

Scilken on the Purpose of the American Public Library

Scilken summarized his philosophy of library service.

My motto is the customer is king. My fundamental belief, and one that librarians
nationally associate me with, is that libraries exist for readers, and we should
serve them with at least some priority. We have a responsibility for the personal
reading of everyone in town.

Libraries are doing too many things. They are slipping away from their
main purpose as the place that makes reading possible all the time. We should,
indeed, go back to the founding purpose of public libraries: to enable people to
read more by quick, free, and easy access to reading material books, magazines,
and newspapers, but mainly books. And to provide help in finding these printed
materials in the library. That's what libraries were all about a hundred years ago,
and that is what we are about today or should be—developing and serving
readers. I'm an old-fashioned librarian. I'm in the book business. My proposal is
to focus on books and reading. We have to sell what we do best. More than ever
we should extol the book.

Most librarians do not read enough, including myself. Some people think
that librarians have read everything in the library and are able to discuss or
explain every book and thus be able to recommend books, new and old. It isn't
always possible to meet those expectations. Most librarians don't know what
books are being read or what the public in a specific community wants. Libraries
don't seem to be interested in what's selling, except for best sellers.

Scilken on Other Services in Public Libraries

I think we are all riding on the backs of readers. If the library did not lend books,
they could not offer all the other services. I have a test that I call the Scilken Test
for All Library Services. If this is the sole service provided by the public library
could you get local tax money to maintain this service? People would say,
'That's not important to us—we don't want our taxes paying for that.'

Scilken admitted that video-lending is another service that might pass the Scilken test. Yet, he added:

Videos and libraries are not, generally speaking, used by the same people, though I guess there's some overlap. I have learned that people who borrow videos are not borrowing books, and people borrowing books are not borrowing videos. They are two separate communities or clienteles. There are five or six factors that will bring new users: a new building, a new director, a major change in the book budget, major changes in hours, and parking.

I tell my colleagues that we are in the book business, not in the information business. To call a public library 'your center for information,' for example, is presumptuous and simply incorrect. It implies that libraries should become Grand Central or Penn Station information booths, with people lined up ready to ask, 'how many people climbed Mount McKinley in 1949?' It is a betrayal of readers, or potential readers, in favor of the library as an information center. The book is thus viewed as a purely utilitarian information resource.

We are having it drummed into us that we are in the information business. I don't think you could have an information bureau standing alone and not lend books. The average person doesn't go to the library for information. The average person turns to friends and colleagues. The average librarian doesn't go to the library if he or she needs information. I don't think people know what librarians are talking about when we refer to libraries as information centers. It's the jargon of our profession but rather meaningless or ambiguous for average people.

It would be interesting to go back and find out where the word 'information,' as a library service, crept into library literature. Somebody ought to make a study of the information sickness that is obsessing libraries. A subject heading or title for the results of this research would be, 'The Transformation of the Library.' My own ad hoc theory is that it comes from the academic world. We've been taught that we librarians are now in the information-dispensing business.

Scilken on Librarian Education

Scilken believed that librarian education has blurred public perceptions of the role of public libraries.

We haven't employed a recent library school graduate in years. For library schools to offer master's degrees they had to introduce a hardware component—technology they call it—to reinforce the perception of public libraries as information centers. It had to be in the curriculum. The schools had to show that libraries are no longer books. So out went the books and reading emphasis and in came technology.

One result is that the library journals are bursting with glossy ads for information-producing machines and gadgetry. And the library schools are influenced by all that advertising and have made technology part of the curriculum, much to the satisfaction of that industry. The schools have to show they are not just interested in books and reading and traditional methods and basic reading literacy. They also began teaching 'information theory,' and that the United States is an information society. I don't understand it. I'm a simplistic thinker.

Librarians will embrace almost any fad, development, or technology, the idea being that they have to keep up with the library Joneses. If the library in the next town has CD-ROMs, we've got to have them, too. If it hires an income-tax expert, well we've got to have one, too.

We need a book renaissance in public libraries and a de-emphasis on technology. Give books a chance to catch up. I think there has been a flight from the book by many librarians. They're embarrassed by books. Librarians embraced almost anything that came down the pike that flees from the book or relegates the book to basement storage. The heavily stocked library book sales are evidence that books are beginning to play second fiddle to information and its technologies. I am not thrilled when I read about technological breakthroughs for information access in libraries.

We are not telling the public what public libraries are about, what they should be doing and what they are doing well. What we do poorly, I think, is not focusing on library patrons—I call them customers—and that should be taught in library schools. When it comes to teaching library public relations, the need for ongoing links with the community is fundamental. Focus on customers. You have to please your customers, who are really local taxpayers. The experienced and the less experienced of us have to know how to keep customers coming back.

Scilken on Public Library Customers

With our limited resources, we should try to satisfy as many needs of as many customers as possible. Still, since public libraries operate on limited amounts of money, we should limit the people we serve and serve them well. It has always struck me as odd that if you don't want to use the library, we'll do anything to get you in, jump through hoops and turn ourselves inside out. It is also true that public libraries cannot serve everyone. We have to define whom we want to serve and do so as well as we can. That should include out-of-school adults, high school students, and senior citizens, preschoolers and elementary grade children—everybody but college students. We should not bother with people who do not want to read. The core mission of the public library is to get as much reading done in the community as possible. Readers are the ones who have the ideas to move the country forward.

I asked Scilken why public libraries should not serve college students.

We should never have to buy books with college students in mind, certainly not as part of our acquisition policy. Most librarians don't know that colleges get $300 or more, on average, from each of their full-time students for library use. Library costs are factored into student fees. Most libraries in the country spend less than $20 per capita or less for public libraries.

We watch our public relations so it is important that we explain to college students why we don't have a book that a university or college library might have. One thing I discovered is that, to the lay person, all libraries are the same-same size buildings and the same books. We give out this letter to students explaining why we can't buy books for courses. They may find helpful materials for general courses in public libraries, but I do not think any public library should make an attempt specifically to serve college students, not for their course work at any rate. For recreational reading, yes. College students are always welcome to join public libraries and borrow what they offer.

Scilken on Public Library Services for Readers

Scilken's policies acknowledged that readers are the primary library patrons. His approach to building the library collection reflected this value. He selected all books, except for reference and children's books. He also personally weeded the stacks.

The libraries' historical mission should be the same today—to concentrate on books and lending. You see, the function of a library is to please our customers. Most librarians don't believe that. What they do is present a core library to their clients and say, 'This is what is important to society. We know what is good for you.' I think all reading is educational: Harlequins, mysteries, westerns, sci-fi. Even the meanest books impart something. It isn't our job to improve the public taste. If some people in Orange want romantic fiction, we supply it.

All books go into circulation within a day or two of receipt. Most books are ordered in advance of publication so that they will be available when reviews appear. This library will try to get any book for a reader. We tell people, just reserve what you wish to read. A patron who wants to buy a book to own may do so through the Orange Public Library Bookstore.

Scilken was also interested in how his library patrons selected their books within the library.

Most public libraries do not have books that people want. People don't like to buy bestsellers. I think it's dumb to turn away or discourage bestseller readers. If you go into the library for a book that everyone else wants, libraries don't care. You may have to wait six months. Well, that's dumb and unfair. No rational business would make people wait a long time to borrow a bestseller. If you ask book readers why they don't use the library, they say the libraries never have anything they would want to read. There have been a thousand, ten thousand, or twenty thousand studies made of public libraries. They ask the same fundamental question: What would you like more of? The suggestion 90 percent of the time is more books, new books. We know that few people are interested in old books.

Yet librarians generally are wary of buying bestsellers, many are at any rate. The problem is that libraries are loath to supply them. They think it's a professional decision not to provide the best sellers or other wanted books. Why are they wary? In the first year of use, every copy of every bestseller in this library and, I suspect, in most libraries will have circulated more than the average book that we throw out. Instead of a life of ten years, it has a life of one year, but has had more circulation in that one year than some other book had over five or ten years. On top of that, it makes people very happy if it meets their needs. They don't want to read the dull book that's going to last ten years or five years. They want to read what they want to read and we have to honor them. That's very important. We have been buying new books for twenty-five years and people still tell me, 'I'm surprised that this book is here because it is new.' Buying multiple copies is cost-effective. It's efficient. There is no better public relations for a library than providing a book a customer wants to read.

Library services are for the here and now. You can't tell what's going to be needed ten years down the pike, but you know what's here now. When I first went into library work, I coined Scilken's First Law of Library Work: Books should be bought for the readers you have before you. Librarians much prefer buying books that nobody wants to books they know everyone wants, or it's better to serve a future reader tomorrow than a reader today.

It is foolish to have a small new-book display. I have found that new books are going to be borrowed while they are displayed, not when not on display. It is more of an invitation to read them when they are in their own area. Some people prefer the look and feel of new books. New books should be kept in their section longer. Once a book leaves our new-book area for older book shelves, it gets much lighter use. We mark the return date in every book we circulate so that I or my staff can go through the new book section and remove books that aren't circulating. We make room for books that are circulating and perhaps buy more copies of books the public wants.

Duplicate copies of popular books are housed in a book-express collection with a three-day circulation period.

Scilken pointed out that the Orange Public Library charges for reserves for new books but reserves for other books are free. Most reserves are filled within thirty days, often earlier.

> Reserves are very important to us because they tell us what can't be found. I wish I could find a way to pay people to put reserves on non-bestsellers. I want to do this because it's better than any survey you could do to find out what you should have in the library. But a lot of people don't like to bother reserving books. I don't think they want to be obligated to come back and pick them up on a certain date.

Orange Public Library patrons provide advice to other readers by writing their opinions in books—on the inside covers, on blank pages, in margins.

> It began when borrowers started putting their initials in books to show that they had read them. In addition people are always looking for good books. Some are desperate for good reading material from among the 120,000 books here. Previous reader evaluations scribbled in books help people decide whether to read a book.

Another way Scilken supported readers was by being strict about overdue books. This policy was described in a red flier illustrated with a parking meter and inscribed, "Don't park overtime with books and other items borrowed from the library." The Orange Public Library's overdue policy was explained in detail: "Overdue notices are expensive to prepare. Return library materials on time—it's cheaper and hassle-free." Under Scilken, the Orange Public Library took strong steps against what it believed may be deliberate refusal to return, discuss, or report overdue books. It asked a collection agency or small-claims court to recover library materials or their value.

Scilken's interpretation of library classification also reflected his service philosophy. He tailored his classification to fulfill readers' needs more quickly. Scilken prepared a marvelously simple "where to find it" guide printed on a single 8.5-by-11-inch sheet. The guide listed 102 subjects in alphabetical order in two columns, from "accounting" to "World War II," with call numbers beside each subject. The reverse side of the sheet gave a floor plan, starting with the lobby and seasonal displays and leading to a hexagon shaped area for new fiction surrounding the circulation desk. This carefully mapped interior geography helped Scilken's staff arrange collections in a logical progression, facilitating patron access.

> What we want to do in public libraries is retail books—something akin to the best retailing systems in supermarkets or department stores, where goods are laid out by categories. We do a bad job of it in libraries. We should not be scattering books on one region of the world, for example, in five places. Most book selection by adults is done after browsing. So what you want to do is enhance browsing—make it as easy as possible to skim through a book or to let it impact on you.

Likewise, Scilken's approach to cataloging emphasized simplicity.

> We offer an easier-to-use catalog. Cards for recent books give important information. The cards have no mysterious abbreviations. Titles are preceded with the word 'title,' subjects with the word 'subject,' authors with the word 'author.' Titles, authors, and subject cards are filed in one alphabet. I think there are aberrational things that are anti-public service that were taught in library schools and one of them is the current application of the Dewey Decimal System. It's an inefficient classification system. I have had discussions with professors at library schools, and it is hopeless. They're tethered to the old system. They say they want books on the same subject in one comprehensive place for easier access. They say that should be done-but they don't do it. What are they waiting for?

Scilken also believed weeding served readers well.

> I will say that most libraries have too many books that no longer justify space on shelves. We weed all the time but I don't weed enough, and most other libraries don't because it is time consuming, difficult, and depressing. We weed our new-book shelves and weed the library generally by how books are circulating. It is harder to weed than to buy a book. When weeding, you have little basis for discarding unless you have a fabulous memory and recall what the reviewers said about a book, good or bad.

Scilken and the Role of the Public Library in Literacy

Scilken was happiest when he found people who read for the joy of it. He believed that libraries were the major creators of good readers in this country.

I think that the only readers in America read as children, using public libraries. I got that idea by talking to people who come into this library day after day. I would ask, 'How did you become a reader?' It is not impossible, but it's not as easy to learn to enjoy reading in later life. Early, voluntary reading of pleasure-giving books is the key to making lifelong readers. You must read a lot of books, hundreds and sometimes thousands of books, from the time you learn to read until you are thirteen. I don't think you can make a reader if children or adults haven't passed through this early reading experience. From this intensive reading experience, children get the connection going in their brains that makes reading part of their lives. They can almost glance at a page and know what's there. Very few people can do that—they struggle and find reading difficult so they don't want to read. A lot of people read for jobs, many read for school and others read for a lot of other reasons. Very few people read voluntarily. The people who read for pleasure are the best readers in America.

I asked Scilken why teaching reading was such a problem in the public schools.

I have a simplistic but, I think, quite accurate answer: TV. I grew up before TV and became an avid reader. Cut out or drastically curtail TV in most American homes and kids have got to turn to books and reading. TV is a tremendous detractor from reading.

In a real sense, the schools and their teachers discourage reading. Many children approach reading in school with dread. Tests and quizzes on books destroy any continuity and pleasure in reading the book. Schools want to help, they want students to read. Their attempts to teach reading helps destroy the joy of reading. Schools couple reading with pain. Schools don't stress pleasure, nor do they stress the potential for joy in losing oneself in book after book. Librarians, on the other hand, say, 'Enjoy the book. We are not going to test you on it.' Librarians don't make the demands on readers that teachers do. So a combination of TV and schools are really not getting the pleasure into reading.

I think we should yield to television what television does best: it imparts facts. What the schools should concentrate on are skills you can't learn by yourself: reading, writing, mathematics, foreign languages, sports, music. It just hurts me that so many kids are labeled failures because they can't absorb or retain things they don't really need to know. That often crowds out things kids should know.

Should public libraries, then, be involved in providing basic literacy?

I think that helping people in their daily lives should be another function of the library, but not the primary function. While one of the most pitiful sights is to see children looking at books they can't read, our assumption has to be that the schools have done their job efficiently and that children and adults coming into the library know how to read.

I don't believe there are many successes in libraries teaching reading. I think that libraries should not be asked to go out and turn nonreaders into readers. That's not our job. It's the job of the schools. It's a hard job, and it's a job for professional reading teachers, not librarians. The idea of dumping this responsibility on libraries is doomed to failure. If we have to teach literacy, the government should pay us for doing that chore. Volunteers teaching English to foreigners in libraries is a cop out by local, state, and federal government. Many foreigners in affluent American towns can well afford paid, experienced instruction. There are a few people who can learn to read as adults, but they are very few. Instead, hard-to-come-by library dollars are used to teach English to foreigners, some of whom are really demanding of library attention. If the schools are failing to teach reading effectively, in many cases, why blame the libraries? If the community wants its library to teach or improve reading, let them appoint a reading consultant or a reading librarian. What libraries should do is take children and give them a start at becoming lifelong readers.

The library profession has also failed to demonstrate the need for children's librarians. It all comes down to a flight from the book to information services at libraries. If we could see the idea that reading is important and that children's librarians are the best-qualified people to get children to read, they will see that libraries are given the money to hire more qualified children's librarians. It will be an investment that society cannot afford to overlook or minimize. It's got to be done. How do we get more children's librarians? Put up the money to make this branch of librarianship desirable. People need to be aware that the library is the only institution—except the family—that creates readers. They need to know that the ability to read gives children one of the most important skills they need in life

Scilken on Public Library Funding

Scilken deplored the disparity of government funding of public libraries. Due to variations in property values and incomes libraries in more affluent areas might spend upwards of $50 per person while libraries in more needful areas may only spend $10 per person.

The public generally thinks libraries get more support than they do. Very few people know the percentage of local budgets that go to into libraries. It runs about 2 percent of local tax revenues. Nobody is going to balance the budget on the backs of the local library because they are not given much money to begin with. You don't cut library services to save money because you save a pittance anyway. It's stupid to cut that amount because it doesn't save you money, and it discourages and prevents thousands of people, especially minorities, from access to reading material. In budget terms, we've never been favored, but I don't think libraries are considered expendable. If libraries have to make cuts they should cut everything that does not deal with books and reading.

This state can and should treat libraries as it does schools and other education institutions. If we had a lot of money, we'd hire professional storytellers, we'd hire children's librarians to go out to the schools, and I'd go out to the parks and do a lot of other things. If I was a library director with more money, I would do more of the same that we are doing here to satisfy the reader. Readers are a precious group in this library.

Scilken on Public Library Promotion

Scilken was a master of library promotion. He used to purchase promotional material produced by library associations but found that his own customized materials were more effective in his library. He believed that society wanted justification for libraries. He was a prolific letter-writer on library issues and often used letters to newspaper editors to expound on library, education and reading issues and to respond to other letters and articles. His letters were regularly published in the *New York Times* and the *Wall Street Journal.*

We can't wait for the American Library Association to communicate about libraries during National Library Week. We've had National Library Week for twenty-five or thirty years, and it's made little impact. They're trying to convert the already converted. One way we can make a contribution to library advancement is to write a letter a week to the media about some aspect of library service. I am one of the few librarians who do that. I try to get an article or letter in every issue of our local paper. Either I write a letter or we encourage other people to do so. *We* have to tell local people what libraries are about, what librarians should be doing and do it well.

Letters, he felt,

are important public relations for libraries that will make an impact at budget time. Not only letters but op-ed articles on one or two of many library issues—financing, non-library use of libraries, building support, the role of libraries in education, libraries for recreational and pleasure reading, books vs. videos and VCRs, whether libraries should be information centers, or whether libraries should take on literacy. Op-ed writing takes time but it's worth it. It's a great service to libraries but the writing has to be good, darn good, if it is to be accepted by the editor. Most newspapers, daily and weekly, are receptive to article and picture ideas. They may not give story suggestions front page, but there will be coverage. Librarians can request a reporter to write up library events and new programs or offer to write them up themselves. Don't only aim for the big dailies. Local weeklies usually have space for library news, and they are distributed free for wide circulation. Address it to the editor by name, not just 'editor,' which suggests junk mail, like 'resident.'

He also encouraged citizens to send letters to editors. Note the verb, send, not write. Scilken saved library patrons the task of composing letters. He had prewritten messages printed on post cards that were distributed at the circulation desk.

I offered prizes, guidelines, and themes to people who would write the best letters about libraries and get them published.
    The other thing that is very important, and the only thing that really matters to librarians, is word of mouth publicity. When people tell their friends and neighbors that 'I found it in the library,' that takes years of doing good to bring that about because libraries have a terrible reputation of not having books that people want.

Scilken believed that public libraries greatest need is to be recognized as important to society.

About 60 percent of the time, municipal profiles in the Sunday real-estate section of the *New York Times* do not mention the local library, although the writer used the library to get information about the community. Yet the towns they pick for articles usually have a lot of people who want library services for pleasure reading and for information. You see, that's another thing that librarians tend to think; that the only people who support libraries are library users and to get support you have to increase library use. Well, I don't think so. I think that we have a great deal of support. People like the idea of libraries but all your users may not be supportive people who want to get enmeshed in library problems. I think we should encourage people to support us, not necessarily to use us. People who don't use libraries nevertheless know that libraries are important in the lives of many people. I think it's more productive to strengthen the support we already have in the community.

My belief is that people don't want to know about the library and its services. I was a member of the local Rotary Club for twenty-five years. There were about forty members, all men, all college graduates, all successful in their professions. Of those forty, only three or four read books, and most of them couldn't be bothered about the library. If they wanted a book, they went out and bought it. They support libraries but do not use them. They bought their own books because they did not want the obligation or pressure of returning library books.

We need supporters. It's time for a bandwagon for reading on which parents and children can jump aboard. Society needs readers. Readers are developed, nurtured, aided, and admired by libraries. They are important to society. Reading is the pathway to a better life. We have the books. We haven't tried to sell that message. There should be reams and reams of testimony from immigrants and young people and old people who use libraries, in part, for success in life and success in school. I am not aware of the existence of comments and quotes praising libraries. It seems to me that somebody, somewhere, should collect library experiences of famous people—life-changing experiences from the availability and use of libraries: the library as a life-changing experience. There must be hundreds of such experiences. I think the idea, by those praised in the press for doing serious reading, is to show the public the roles of the public library in the lives of prominent persons. The public approves of people who are serious readers. They like to think of their leaders as book readers. One of the few services that the middle class uses voluntarily and extensively are libraries. The middle class doesn't need to be told how important libraries are. They know it.

Scilken had long been adept at writing slogans. He printed them, among other places, on library envelopes. Here are a few: "Preventing illiteracy by promoting the joy of reading," "Ask for any book," "The library receives about two cents of the local tax dollar." He believed that it was "time for librarians to really sound off at rallies and meetings."

Scilken believed, however, that such rallies and meetings should lead to tangible results at the local library level. When asked about the effectiveness of the second White House Conference on Libraries, Scilken replied:

Librarians have got to stop being thrilled at the idea of a White House Conference. If the last White House Conference had a point, it escaped me. White House Conferences are often totally unnoticed by the media and therefore by 99 percent of the people of this country. They passed a lot of resolutions but nothing that affected the operation of this library in Orange, New Jersey, in terms of financial support, operations, or procedures. There were a few generalizations about the need for readers and silly posters showing show-business types holding books. I would say that 99 percent of other public libraries were not affected one iota by the first White House Conference. If the main purpose of the White House Conference was to generate good publicity for public libraries, it failed miserably. The best thing it did was to enable the White House to make friends with a lot of key librarians. The people who were there loved it, without exception. You would have to be darned stupid to mount another one. I have to conclude that the conferences were set up to give First Ladies something to do, like dedicating ships by hitting them with bottles of champagne or reading to children in photo opportunities.

I think the American Library Association and the state library associations and librarians should focus on one theme. Every year, the American Library Association comes up with a new slogan to confuse it. The problem is that we are too diffuse. Libraries are too spread out to take a yearly slogan from the White House or library associations and make something of it. A slogan that is used for five to ten years will be more effective than having to promote a new one every year. A yearly slogan won't sink in. Scarcely does one get quoted, adopted, and remembered than we have to contend with a new one. We can't run libraries by sloganeering. Libraries have a story to tell, and we haven't told it. We are not selling too well. We don't want to increase use. What we want to do is show the social values of libraries.

Library associations seem to prefer to deal with a lot of internal things that do not involve the public. This includes library classification systems, the price of journals, and book selection, all topics that do not engage the public. My point is that their public relations focus is wrong.

Scilken's advice extended to changing the image of the librarian. This image needed to change from that of a

well-meaning, ineffectual person to somebody important to society. Who can do that and how is that done? By experienced public-relations people. It will cost money to influence and rally broad public opinion, politicians, government officials, and legislatures to help protect public libraries.

Scilken's Legacy to the Community of Orange, New Jersey

"They ought to put up a statue of Marvin in front of the library for what he did, and is doing, for this city," said Felice C. Spagno, an executive secretary in Orange. Scilken was described as a maverick, a know-it-all, as brash, supremely self-confident, down-to-earth, as a living legend, and as an iconoclast, and a breath of gale-force fresh air in an often stodgy profession. Call him what you will, Scilken was an effective and provocative spokesman on library issues and policies. He was probably more influential than his professional colleagues cared to admit. In this interview he sounded off on almost every issue facing American public libraries.

Chapter 7

Scilken Aphorisms

Loriene Roy

Perhaps the most important information in the *U*N*A*B*A*S*H*E*D Librarian* were the many notes, reflections, and comments that Marvin H. Scilken inserted into his quarterly. This chapter presents over four hundred quotes attributed to Marvin, the majority of which are drawn from issues of the *U*N*A*B*A*S*H*E*D Librarian*. Quotations are presented chronologically under broad subject headings.

In 1994, Marvin Scilken asked, "has anyone compiled a list of library/reader/book quotation books?"[1] Some twenty-five years later, we see that Marvin, in essence, created such a reference source.

American Library Association

1.   For the record, I think the ALA should be a professional organization with *formal* relations with trustees and arms length relations with publishers.[2]
2.   Only librarians, and people working in libraries, should be in the ALA.[3]

Author–Library Relations

3.   I think libraries ought to charge unknown authors for the service public libraries provide for them.[4]
4.   Libraries build audiences for authors.[5]

5. Libraries help authors by keeping their books available for years, helping authors find their audience.[6]
6. After reading a book or article, we should write the authors with the suggestion that they acknowledge their use of libraries.[7]

Authors and Readers

7. Writers are readers first.[8]

Book of the Month Club

8. The fact that bookstores and the Book of the Month Club are in business, I consider a failure to the library operation. If we were really good, we would have their customers.[9]

Book Design

9. A book should look and feel good in the hand.[10]

Book Displays

10. Libraries lose a lot of circulation by not displaying new books.[11]

Book Reviews

11. When using the Sunday *New York Times Book Review* the popularity of a book is generally inversely related to the length of the review (double the ratio for front page reviews).[12]
12. There are three factors to consider in buying books: the text, the "package," and the cost (not price). Reviews should deal with all three.[13]
13. I have found an inverse relation between the length of review and popularity of the book—generally speaking. The books with the very small reviews are the most popular.[14]

Books—Marketing

14. I guess the rule is what's selling *everywhere* is a faulty guide to what's selling *anywhere*.[15]
15. Public librarians know that many books are judged by their covers (and blurbs).[16]

16. I consider ads "my friend."[17]
17. Generally, the larger the ad the higher the publisher's expectation for a title.[18]
18. I have never met a human being who bought an un-hyped first novel.[19]
19. If we are to merchandise old books, they have to be in the best possible condition.[20]
20. Publishers don't usually advertise books that aren't selling. They believe in mercy death—books that aren't selling, aren't advertised.[21]

Bookstores

21. The ratio of desired books to undesired books favors the book store.[22]

Browsing

22. Generations of indoctrination by librarians have left library users so dependent on the catalog that they don't browse widely or intensively enough to discover how much material is widely scattered and accessible only through browsing.[23]
23. Encouraging the fullest exploration of library resources means shifting our emphasis from the pigeon-holing of individual books to the organization of large amounts of material for easy exploration.[24]
24. Browsers don't always go out with what they came for, but they're more likely to go out with something.[25]
25. The primacy of browsing obviously has implications for networking, book selection, speed of acquisition, loan periods, cataloging, classification, condition of the book, and display.[26]
26. Half the fun in a library is falling across the unexpected.[27]
27. From the point of view of a browser, and most of adult public library book users are browsers, does it matter if a book is "mis-shelved" (that is, shelved away from other books on the same subject) following Dewey 20 or accidentally mis-shelved by a patron or page.[28]

Catalog Use

28. It is my observation that many clients may catch words out of a title and look for the book by these catchwords.[29]

Cataloging

29. Librarians insist on cluttering catalogs with unused, and therefore unneeded, entries.[30]

30. What is needed is a public library cataloging institute to create cataloging for the "real" world.[31]
31. In our quest for professionalism, we have managed to make our catalogs less intelligible to many users.[32]
32. We should devote some of our intelligence to making our catalogs intelligible to casual users.[33]
33. I doubt a librarian can catalog well or face the public without knowing a lot about a lot of things.[34]
34. The medium being the message, we might match our card type style to the book at hand.[35]

Catalogs

35. It is my feeling that the card catalog is a mystery to most people.[36]
36. Many public and school libraries do not need the catalog card paraphernalia that research libraries feel they need.[37]
37. It is my belief that we head many potential users off at the catalog.[38]
38. For good or bad, catalogs are one of library's main distinguishing characteristics.[39]
39. I have the naive approach that our catalogs (card, book, or microform) should be able to be as easily understood by real people as are those of Sears Roebuck or the telephone company.[40]
40. Scilken's gut law of add on, supplemental, and/or divided catalogs: a reader's chance of locating a desired work in a catalog is inversely proportional to the cube of the number of places to look.[41]

Classification

41. Is there a real need to have an absolutely consistent classification?[42]
42. My words to the Dewey people: *"old numbers for old subjects, new numbers for new subjects."*[43]
43. All that matters *to readers* is that they find all the library's books on the same subject in one place.[44]
44. The DDC now is a thing of beauty and an expense forever.[45]
45. While the Dewey office is organizing knowledge, the rest of us are retailing books.[46]
46. [A] terrible thing that has happened to the library profession is the constant changing of the Dewey decimal system.[47]
47. The tolerance of the library community to changing classification numbers is a mockery of library "science."[48]
48. The changing of classification numbers to achieve an aesthetic organization of ever-changing knowledge seems to me to be at odds with our desire to merchandise books.[49]
49. I was telling a visiting colleague that to "merchandise" (to use current jargon) books the most important function of a cataloger is to classify books

where most readers will stumble on them, since many (most) users don't use the catalog or don't use it the way we think they should.[50]

50. Librarians who, in the name of efficiency and cost effectiveness, take books from the book process or box, or whose catalogers merely copy the Dewey classification numbers supplied by the Library of Congress, are hiding many books from many users.[51]

51. If I were the director of a public library I would work to bring books together on the shelf that common sense would bring together.[52]

52. Classification may be the most important thing that a public oriented librarian does.[53]

Continuing Education

53. Certainly much news is "junk news," time-eating, filling, not nutritious and maybe harmful, but still necessary for a librarian's "diet" to cope with public interests.[54]

54. I learn something from every library I visit.[55]

Copyright

55. The public seems to have lost a lot under the new copyright law. Journal publishers seem to have gotten to erect toll booths at information transfer points charging both authors and users and anyone who happens to pass by.[56]

Education for Librarianship

56. Perhaps we would have served our publics better if we had founded library schools in close association with colleges of retailing.[57]

57. [Required Courses for Professional Librarians.] One Upmanship for Librarians, or How to Answer a Question While Putting Down the Questioner.[58]

58. Epidemic of library school closings is a symptom of the fast declining status of librarians.[59]

Fiction

59. Fiction provides windows to worlds many never see and never want to see.[60]

60. Libraries need a defense for fiction.[61]

Fines

61. "Image" may be another reason for having substantial fines; obviously an organization can't be worth much if it deals in picayune amounts—pennies.[62]
62. Either have high fines or no fines—there is no "image" middle ground.[63]

Interlibrary Loan

63. Scilken's observation of professional satisfaction: one interlibrary loan is worth one hundred circulations.[64]

Librarians—Personal Narratives

64. I regret I did not keep a diary.[65]

Library Aims and Objectives

65. Libraries still remain passive monuments to Victorian high seriousness—half warehouse, half study-hall.[66]
66. We are not organizing knowledge, we are retailing books.[67]
67. Give the people what they want. It's their library.[68]
68. Because of the observable great disparity in (1) funding, (2) holdings, and (3) purposes, I don't think distinctions are blurring or even could blur between types of libraries.[69]
69. Public libraries' first priority should be those who have no other library funded to serve them.[70]
70. I believe, that for our society to prosper, it's important to lessen the difference in library service between rich and poor communities.[71]
71. Many librarians in power seem to be embarrassed by small libraries.[72]
72. Libraries should focus on books, reading and literacy.[73]
73. We have to refine our message in this age of literacy and identify ourselves primarily with books.[74]
74. The credit [libraries] deserve is to be recognized as the center of intellectual activity in the scholarly community.[75]
75. If the university is the womb of our culture, maybe libraries should be thought of as the placenta and umbilical cord, nurturing and carrying knowledge to students and faculty and ultimately to the world at large.[76]
76. Wal-Marts don't provide library service.[77]
77. No matter what role(s) we espouse, the central theme of public libraries should be terrific book service to readers, adults, and children.[78]
78. The basic constant is books.[79]

79. Public libraries have been and ought to continue to be a basic service of government.[80]
80. In these days with superstores and Internet competition we have to restore our credibility.[81]
81. Libraries are in the book business.[82]
82. The Scilken Observation: to much of the public, all libraries are the same size and have the same things.[83]
83. To many, a library is a library is a library.[84]
84. The library is more than information.[85]

Library Forms

85. I have an emotional feeling (irrational I know) that forms can make libraries perform.[86]

Library Safety Measures

86. To discourage untoward happenings in library restrooms, I have suggested airplane-sized restrooms.[87]

Library Circulation and Loan

87. One of the main benefits of automated circulation systems is the easy qualification (or rather the disqualification) of borrowers.[88]
88. While we can't eliminate "reserves" for happenstance books, we can minimize most reserves for books that we *know* will be wanted.[89]
89. It seems to this observer that automated circulation systems are purchased for status and neatness.[90]
90. Libraries should be chary of pressuring nonusers into borrowing, because adult never-before borrowers may not be willing to play the library game by returning books.[91]
91. By cajoling people into using libraries we may convert "passive likers" into "active dislikers" after receiving a friendly overdue note or two.[92]
92. Selling library use is not like selling soap because there are two parts to library activity: items must be borrowed and returned.[93]
93. Libraries can only economically serve those who are willing to return borrowed items.[94]
94. Sharing is the basis of library service.[95]
95. Copies of best sellers usually have short intensive lives, being borrowed many times in a short period of time. It's been my observation that most other books never achieve the same number of uses per copy in the years they remain on the shelf.[96]
96. I've reached the conclusion that a high portion of the adult circulation at many public libraries is generated from books less than two years or so old.[97]

97. I find that every copy of our popular books receive far more circulation before they are discarded than the vast majority of the library's other books. The difference is that they achieve this use during their first year.[98]

98. It's very distressing but informative to see books that one had high hopes for to be little used.[99]

99. It's very difficult to get some people to become regular library users. There are many reasons, but certainly two are time limits and fines.[100]

100. Now that books are easily available in superstores and the Internet, we have to find some way of reducing our annoyance factors.[101]

101. Does it pay to entice non-users, who probably think nice things about the library, to borrow something, then humble them with overdue notices.[102]

102. Determine if there are any discernible patterns in your overdues.[103]

103. First time users: send reminders *before* items are due.[104]

104. For items not in demand let borrowers in good standing set their own reasonable due dates.[105]

105. Reduce the fear of using libraries and don't turn borrowers into enemies. Remember we have lost our monopolies.[106]

106. The most important time of a book's life is when it is new.[107]

107. Libraries should encourage reserves for books that they don't expect to get, the reserves will help the library to find holes in the collection.[108]

Library Evaluation

108. Public libraries should be one of the most effective cost benefit educational (and recreational) institutions in the world.[109]

109. Libraries fulfill various roles in communities' psyches. In some situations it may be worthwhile to look around to see what may be perceived as lavish.[110]

110. Poor or unresponsive library service may make taxpayers critical of government in general.[111]

111. The library's economic impact may be likened to having a very large employer in town.[112]

112. In many communities the most used government "voluntary" service is libraries.[113]

113. Readers finding their own books on the shelf is what makes economic library operation possible.[114]

114. I have suggested to researchers that a reading "timeline" be established by compiling a "Scilken R1" similar to the Federal Reserve Bank's "M1." The "Scilken R1" would consist of a grand total annually for:

1. Library circulation;
2. Book sales;
3. Newspaper circulation; and
4. Magazine circulation.[115]

115. Public libraries usually provide more beneficial public contact per dollar of tax money than any other public service.[116]

116. Libraries may be the most cost effective (and inexpensive) educational bargain around.[117]

117. The obverse of a "cost:benefit" ratio is a "savings:harm" ratio. The small amount of money "saved" will generate enormous ill-will towards County government in thousands of influential people.[118]

118. Libraries, one of the most inexpensive public services in most places, build repeat traffic for area merchants because borrowers must return regularly to bring back their books.[119]

119. Always use questions on voting when conducting surveys. Elected officials should be interested in services used by voters.[120]

120. Some studies have shown that propinquity is a major factor in library use.[121]

121. Public librarians want everyone to use the library because it's the American way of demonstrating success.[122]

122. In their localities libraries are monopolies.[123]

Library Finance

123. As far as libraries are concerned society is willing to spend more on the preparation for life than on life itself. That is, we'll spend all kinds of money to teach students to do research so that they are prepared to do research as citizens, but don't give enough money to public libraries to enable citizens to pursue "research."[124]

124. We should remember that library *use* and library *service* have only a sometime relationship to library *support*.[125]

125. Without book readers there would, I believe, be scant library support.[126]

126. Much public library public relations attempt to increase library use, partly in the belief that increased use will insure support.[127]

127. I'll bet that the public does not know what percentage of local taxes is devoted to libraries.[128]

128. Libraries where voters vote directly on library budgets generally do very well indeed.[129]

129. The idea that library service is free and somehow exists without its being a cost to anyone inhibits libraries from getting adequate funding.[130]

130. One reason public libraries frequently have difficulty getting financial support is the confusion and diffusion of library roles.[131]

131. I believe that if we give terrific book service and engage the passions of readers, we will get enough money to do many of the other things we like to do, but all is balanced on book service.[132]

132. If there's a public library convenient to Main Street, make sure it has enough money to stay open.[133]

133. It seems to me that there are three factors about public libraries that should be of help in securing funding.
> 1. Most *voters* use libraries.
> 2. They are inexpensive.
> 3. They do many good things.[134]

134. Library service should not be anonymously funded.[135]

135. People should know where library funds come from.[136]

136. We need to communicate libraries' vast popularity to *the key funder.*[137]

137. Libraries are perhaps the most inexpensive of all tax-funded educational endeavors.[138]

138. We tell all who will listen, "library service is priceless," then we price it low.[139]

139. Our job is to convince local people to spend local money on quality library service.[140]

140. Perhaps a way to get better public libraries in places that need them the most would be to dedicate a percentage of school aid to the libraries.[141]

141. Many librarians deal with public funds and it is our duty to the public and funders to get the best value possible.[142]

142. Ask; you may receive.[143]

143. Libraries in many municipalities are positioned in the funding drain far too low; they are rarely perceived as essential.[144]

144. In my view librarians, by embracing the idea that they *should* raise large amounts of private money, have vastly diminished the status of public libraries as worthy of tax support.[145]

145. Avoid gifts that will raise operating costs.[146]

146. The biggest factor in budgets is usually last year's budget.[147]

147. I thought if elected officials knew that voters considered libraries important they would fund them more eagerly.[148]

Library History

148. The Carnegie Corporation should institute a group to look into the establishment of a library museum, to honor libraries and Andrew Carnegie.[149]

Library Marketing Slogans

149. The public library is an institution that can help deinstitutionalize people.[150]

150. The library is important to people who are important to the city.[151]

151. The library—the people's book club.[152]

152. The library—the thinking people's book club.[153]

153. The library—the smart people's book club.[154]

154. Libraries are where the voters are.[155]

155. Look smart, carry a book. Be smart, carry a *library* book.[156]

156. Libraries are stalls in the marketplace of ideas.[157]

157. Preventing illiteracy by promoting the *joy* of reading.[158]

158. The library keeps reading alive.[159]

159. The library enhances the quality of life.[160]

160. Libraries are environmentally "correct." (We recycle culture.)[161]

161. I believe our major message to politicians would be that "libraries are more than a 'good thing,' libraries are important to people who are important to you."[162]

162. If newspapers are to have readers tomorrow they should support libraries today.[163]

163. Public libraries truly add to the quality of our lives.[164]

164. Most voters are library users.[165]

Library Networks

165. Any savings to be had from the "sharing of resources" might be overwhelmed by the costs of networking.[166]

166. In networking: necessity is the mother of convention.[167]

167. Uncompensated reciprocal borrowing asserts the right to plunder other libraries for books.[168]

168. Uncompensated borrowing is unjust, unrealistic, financially unsound and discourages library funding.[169]

169. One of the many glories of American libraries is their ability to borrow books they don't own from libraries that own them for readers needing a specific title.[170]

Library of Congress

170. What's good for LC may not be good for all of us smaller libraries.[171]

Library Personnel Management

171. Libraries must move up to employ more people to render really nifty, positive, socially important service.[172]

172. Any library that can afford it should have an actual human answering their phone.[173]

Library Public Relations

173. I have felt for a long time that one of public libraries' public relations' major theme should be what great and not so great people have used the public library to accomplish something.[174]

174. With every large and small event honored by a commemorative stamp one wonders where the library is in the national psyche when ALA cannot get a stamp celebrating its one hundred years of existence.[175]

175. Most libraries should stress libraries' inexpensiveness.[176]

176. Everything we do should look good but not slick.[177]

177. With an apparent surplus of librarians, shouldn't librarians redirect their scholarship monies to a public education campaign stressing the worth of

libraries to our societies. When the public is convinced, we'll need scholarships again.[178]

178. Libraries have rarely focused their meager public relations efforts properly.[179]

179. Library public relations should be devoted to creating library supporters.[180]

180. In these times of taxpayer uneasiness, it's good to identify what taxes did *not* pay for.[181]

181. Since libraries are used over and over again they have more positive "voter contact" than any (most) other discretionary services.[182]

182. Library use should be voluntary. Let there be no lures.[183]

183. Step back and look at your operations. You are probably doing something other libraries would like to know about.[184]

184. Anything that brings people into the library I believe is a help to the library.[185]

185. The easy availability of wanted books is the best public relations a library could have.[186]

186. P.R. alone will not bring in many new users.[187]

187. We owe it to the public and we owe it to our libraries to write columnists, newspapers, magazines, etc., whenever we have the opportunity. This will help raise our visibility and let nonusers know we are doing "good things."[188]

188. It is, of course, also the very best public relations when a library can supply a wanted book immediately.[189]

189. Every story can be a library story.[190]

190. When writing newspapers I frequently end my letters with the note: "libraries need all the credit they deserve."[191]

191. Our flight from books and reading defuses our messages and image.[192]

192. Let's try to put some continuity and unity into library public relations.[193]

193. Library staff could raise library visibility by writing letters to the press at every opportunity.[194]

194. I believe we have to "sell" libraries at every opportunity.[195]

195. Libraries' messages have to be consistent, continuing, and focused.[196]

196. One way to get the attention of movers and shakers is to invite them to speak at library meetings.[197]

197. Communications from users are far more credible and therefore effective than communication from staff.[198]

198. Our problem is to get adult library users to support libraries as NRA members support guns.[199]

199. I am always seeking ideas that will help libraries get decent funding and recognition.[200]

200. All of us interested in libraries should write every time we see a library *hook*.[201]

201. These library-dependent firms should create infomercials boosting libraries.[202]

202. ALA should find a way to encourage scriptwriters to include favorable library situations in TV soaps and sitcoms and motion pictures.[203]

203. I'm always seeking ways to boost the importance of reading and books.[204]

204. Because publishers and library organizations don't seem to be interested in promoting reading at the present time, I suggest and urge all of us who believe that a reading public is essential, use what we have at hand and engage in sustained letter writing campaigns, extolling the importance of reading to the individual and society.[205]

205. America is ambivalent about its libraries.[206]

206. There are very very few national campaigns telling the library story.[207]

207. We should all take time to tell of the good that librarians and libraries do.[208]

208. I am a library-boosting letter writer.[209]

209. In their public relations arsenal the public library world needs a book of well-known people who credit their success to the public library.[210]

210. In my view, public relations should be geared to solidifying support of non- and probably never-will-be users.[211]

211. I believe libraries, librarians, and state libraries have to sell the case for libraries everyday in every possible way.[212]

212. Too often libraries are overlooked. Their omnipresence leads to invisibility.[213]

213. Most librarians believe the visibility of libraries and librarians needs to be increased.[214]

214. We should give elected officials reasons to support public libraries rather than giving them reasons not to support public libraries.[215]

215. Make the public aware the more money a library receives the more it can do.[216]

216. Libraries are the Rodney Dangerfield of America's educational world. They are frequently not supported and often not thought of.[217]

217. Libraries usually don't get the status they deserve.[218]

218. We all should work to "get libraries the credit they deserve."[219]

219. It's always been my object to marry elected officials to the library.[220]

220. I am always looking for a hook to publicize the library's role.[221]

Library Science Periodicals

221. I guess the death of a major library publication is only another small indication of the decline of the United States.[222]

Library Services

222. The first example of Scilken's Law that sloth brings its own reward: if you are slow enough in providing a wanted service you can charge twice for it.[223]

223. Libraries, I believe, have an opportunity to show their usefulness to library nonusers (and users) by emphasizing consumer information.[224]

224. We have studies that show what "the public" wants; but we take the results as an affront to our professionalism and ignore the conclusions.[225]

225. Books, I believe, are the essence of public library service.[226]

226. The Scilken Test should be applied to library programs: if the program in question were the *only* thing the library did, would *local* funds be available for it?[227]

227. No matter how much we wish to identify ourselves with other services, we should pay attention to our basic business—the book business.[228]

228. I believe that libraries should not engage in many additional programs until they have established excellent traditional service in books and reference.[229]

229. Many state policies seem to ignore the need for libraries to be near the people.[230]

230. The public library is a good place to start when one wants to find out about almost anything.[231]

231. A major problem is, we feel better about ourselves and our role in society when we find an answer to an "intellectual" question by a college student than we do when we answer some consumer questions or provide a Harlequin romance or bestseller to an avid reader.[232]

232. It's our jobs, but it's the users' service.[233]

233. Libraries will have to meet the competition of superstores and the Internet by really super service in supplying books and other media-in-demand.[234]

234. If public library service is inadequate there should be someone to blame.[235]

235. Books are basic.[236]

Library Services for Students

236. Too often libraries are associated with pain and suffering by students doing assignments.[237]

237. Public libraries should not be penalized for not having titles college students can't find or choose not to use at their college libraries.[238]

238. It is unseemly for colleges to take tuition money for courses and not make books *conveniently* available for their students, sending them foraging at their public libraries.[239]

239. Many college students seem to feel libraries of any size are the *same* size and should have most of the books they need.[240]

240. It seems pretty clear to me that college students are public library abusers when they attempt to use public libraries for their curriculums.[241]

241. Few public libraries have the financial support to give meaningful service to college students while still serving members of the general public who have no other library funded to serve them.[242]

242. Teachers should be reminded that libraries work on the average demand principle, that is, they rarely have large quantities of the same book or books on the same person or subject.[243]

243. It's very depressing when students learn the lesson that the library doesn't have what a teacher said the library had.[244]

Library Thefts

244. Under the law of the conservation of library losses, library losses will tend to remain constant no matter what.[245]

245. Libraries would get more books back if they had obvious and hard-to-remove property marks.[246]

246. Unlike hotel towels, many people are loathe to have "overdue" library books in their homes.[247]

Library Users

247. There seems to be a vast difference between people who borrow books from the public library and people who borrow popular records.[248]

248. The overwhelming number of people who use public libraries use libraries for book-related activities.[249]

249. Most libraries with reasonable support are probably serving almost everyone in the community who is near enough and is willing to put up with them.[250]

250. The demographics of library users and voters overlap.[251]

251. I believe that every public library establishes an equilibrium with users. Assuming stable demographics, traffic patterns, and parking, that equilibrium will not change unless the library makes major *internal* changes.[252]

252. In my observation a library only increases its use by building a new building or changing directors.[253]

253. I have never met a new regular user who, seeing a library slogan, "discovered" the library.[254]

254. With all the money spent on student service, shouldn't libraries try to channel their efforts to users who have no other library to serve them.[255]

255. New users in one's community are difficult to get.[256]

256. Building a new building and changing directors (which usually inaugurates a new buying policy) or changing hours seem to be the only ways to attract new users.[257]

257. Most libraries have all the members they are ever going to get.[258]

258. [Library users are] willing to play your game, to put up with you—bring books back on time and generally do what you want them to do.[259]

259. The day-to-day adult public library user would find few things s/he would care to read in a college library.[260]

260. Should we thank our anonymous good borrowers just for making the library possible and our lives livable? [261]

261. I note out-of-school adults use very few books used by high school students and students use few books used by out-of-school adults. It's as if we had two libraries shelved and cataloged as one.[262]

262. I encounter very very few out-of-school adults doing research other than consumer-type lookups.[263]

263. Over the years I have noticed that the demographics of library users was very similar to the demographics of voters.[264]

264. Elected officials should value libraries because they are used by people who can return them to office or turn them out. [265]

265. With our scarce resources, isn't it fair and logical to believe public libraries owe their best efforts to those residents who have no other library funded to serve them?[266]

266. Libraries' most important public is people who fund us.[267]

267. For many voters public libraries are their only regular contact with local and state government.[268]

268. We are all riding on the back of the mystery reader.[269]

269. Information seekers may make very few trips to libraries while borrowers return time and again.[270]

270. We have to find ways to keep our users.[271]

271. If you spend time on the floor you know the borrower.[272]

Management Theory Maxims

272. There are very few really new ideas in the library world; there has been much reinventing.[273]

273. The important thing about ideas is that be useful and not in common practice.[274]

274. Almost every library has some "nifty" idea that saves them (and can save others) time or money, or provides better service.[275]

275. The greatest factor in human affairs is inertia. Let's get going.[276]

276. There seems to be no end to the inventiveness of librarians.[277]

277. Every once in a while some library disease sweeps through libraryland like an epidemic. These diseases I call Cocktail Party Contagion where librarians cannot feel comfortable unless they have the latest, no matter what the cost.[278]

278. Some imaginative writer might do a paper on the "Harmful Effects of Conferences in the Quick Dissemination of Costly Ideas."[279]

279. We should do nothing that may be perceived as squandering public funds.[280]

280. How can we play at solving future library problems when we don't know where the bucks go now.[281]

281. I get the feeling from time to time that many public libraries are run for the inconvenience of their patrons.[282]

282. Check your bills.[283]

283. A major advantage of small and medium-sized libraries is the ability to have "management" close to the customer.[284]
284. Good ideas are recycled all the time.[285]
285. I came to believe that every director could run a better library with some weekly floor-walking experience.[286]
286. We need intelligence even more than we need coordination.[287]

Materials Selection

287. It is ironic that we tell consumers that libraries are a source of consumer information, but we have very little hard information for our own purchases.[288]
288. Purchasing multiple copies violates Scilken's First Empirical Law of Librarians' Science. Librarians much prefer buying books no one wants, to buying books that they know everyone wants, or, it's better to serve a possible reader later than to serve an actual reader now.[289]
289. Librarians use much verbiage, effort, and even some money on so-called public relations trying to convince patrons that they should think well of an institution that rarely seems to have what they want until the desire for it has disappeared.[290]
290. As things are now, with book budgets forming a comparatively minor portion of most public libraries' expenditures, it is good business and not very expensive to have the best kind of public relations—the books![291]
291. The collection at many public libraries consists of the unwanted, the unpopular, and the unstolen.[292]
292. Though it may be inconsistent with some of our professional ideas it might be useful to establish the idea that librarians act as "agents" for the public in the selection of materials.[293]
293. If professional securities selectors cannot do better than chance, can professional book selectors do better than chance?[294]
294. Book selection is people selection.[295]
295. Isn't it more important to spend limited resources on books rather than records of books.[296]
296. Taxpayers may not understand a library's need for multiple copies so we do not like to show more than two copies of any title in any one public shelving area.[297]
297. Make room for younger bestsellers.[298]
298. As I see book selection, I have two objects: to get the most use for dollars spent and to buy books that will be read (and avoid books that won't be read).[299]
299. The purchase of bestsellers is a most efficient use of library funds.[300]
300. Bestsellers can be cost effective "friends" if we let them.[301]
301. We should junk the term "collection" and use the British phrase "book stock."[302]
302. From now on, "stock management," not collection development.[303]

303. It's ironic that librarians who pride themselves on providing information to others are so *information poor* when it comes to buying books, their most frequent purchase.[304]

304. From a cost-per-circulation point of view, multiple copies of popular books are a "best buy" and they make readers very happy and boost the morale of the circulation staff.[305]

305. I always look for books and authors mentioned in the media. Since they are in public view the mentioned books might be read.[306]

306. Keep buying wanted books until they start appearing on the shelf.[307]

307. Libraries don't return books that don't "sell."[308]

308. Actually I believe that libraries should get better (higher) discounts than bookstores because libraries don't return books—returns are *very* expensive for all concerned.[309]

309. A sale to a library is a real sale, not a consignment.[310]

310. Public libraries are the kennels of the publishers' dogs.[311]

Nonresident Users

311. Libraries have sold their services too cheaply.[312]

312. The setting of nonresident fees presents an opportunity to tell the public what library service costs and what it's worth.[313]

313. In my opinion public libraries should set nonresident fees as high as possible. We tell the world our services are very valuable. Yet when we price ourselves we tend to set low prices.[314]

314. The fairest nonresident fee per person would be the library's budget divided by the number of registered borrowers. The result would be what it costs to serve a borrower.[315]

315. The library community has a dilemma. We tell people that library service is so valuable, it's priceless. Yet when we actually price our services, such as for nonresident cards, we frequently price it below the actual cost of serving a borrower.[316]

316. We should figure the charge of our nonresident cards in the same manner that many school districts compute out-of-district tuition: total budget divided by number of students.[317]

317. In our desire to bring library service to everyone libraries frequently set low nonresident fees.[318]

Outsourcing

318. I've not prognosticated well but it seems to me that outsourced public library management and outright privatization will make its profits by eroding the pay, status, and perquisites of library professional and non-professional staff.[319]

319. Privatization means that profit has replaced love as the driving force of service.[320]

Publishers

320. We have a symbiotic relationship with publishers and authors—for public libraries buy books the public chooses not to buy. If we did not buy them they would not be published.[321]

321. Since libraries and schools have been *the* country's major buyers of trade juvenile books, one would think that publishers would do everything possible to help libraries to attract children to books.[322]

322. It's a continuing *scandal* that ALA or the publishing industry has never set standards for so-called "publishers" library bindings.[323]

323. Libraries may be viewed as a subsidy to the book industry.[324]

324. Beware that many publishers offer low discounts to libraries, apparently in the belief that they have *a right* to more profit when selling to nonprofit institutions.[325]

325. Many trade publishers don't give libraries a fair shake in the marketplace.[326]

326. Instead of libraries subsidizing publishers, perhaps publishers should subsidize libraries for the services they perform in maintaining and enlarging America's book-reading public.[327]

327. Librarians don't always seize the opportunity provided by publishers by making books that borrowers ask for available to them, without subjecting them to unreasonable waits.[328]

328. Trade publishing is so popular a business, in my view, because it is heavily subsidized by libraries.[329]

329. Publishers generally want to make a lot of money and librarians generally want to do good.[330]

330. Many publishers who "understand" the library market exploit our desire to do good and earn unconscionable profits.[331]

331. I am mystified why more publishers don't help libraries; in addition to helping society, it builds their future.[332]

332. Publishers have, for the most part, left it up to us in the public sector to promote reading.[333]

Readers

333. Most readers read for pleasure.[334]

334. Many readers read for the pleasure of informing themselves.[335]

335. Very few readers read "through" a subject.[336]

336. I have the feeling that most good readers had access to large numbers of books when they first began to read on their own.[337]

337. My experience indicates that readers read for information in the same way joggers run for transportation.[338]

338. Many librarians do not believe that most book readers read for pleasure (self-fulfillment).[339]

339. I view American society as an inverted pyramid. We all depend on the thoughtfulness of informed *readers* at the apex.[340]

Readers' Services

340. Why are we surprised, then, when other people prefer to buy books than conform to our time schedules. [341]

341. We are spending all sorts of money on data bases and computer networks to serve the unusual library user while the person who wants the book just reviewed can't get it for all sorts of "good" reasons.[342]

342. If public libraries are going to be institutions of mass culture we have to find out what the masses can use us for and nurture the people who read, even if they read *True Story*, Harlequin books, and *The Pirate*.[343]

343. As inflation rages, public libraries should be able to pick up a few more customers; higher prices should make library rules acceptable to more book readers.[344]

344. The least expensive service a library provides happens when a reader finds a wanted book on the shelf, takes it out, and returns it on or near the time due.[345]

345. Libraries must stress reading for pleasure to reach the large public that reads for pleasure.[346]

346. Many librarians feel better giving the Theory of Relativity to a serious reader than making available a romance to another reader.[347]

347. It seems to make us feel better about ourselves when readers want serious books.[348]

348. Attracting new readers to a library is difficult. A library's best bet is getting present book readers to use the library.[349]

349. There appears to be a flight [among librarians] from the book.[350]

350. Many books have lives briefer than a fruitfly. Getting the book to the reader while it is still in season is one key to a successful library.[351]

351. Most public libraries with decent book budgets can supply *all* requests for popular books within a maximum wait of one month, if they really want to.[352]

352. Public libraries have to emphasize reading for the sheer joy of reading if America will have book readers in the future.[353]

353. We should give first-class service to people who are eager to read books.[354]

354. Many library leaders seem to suffer from librophobia.[355]

355. All our programs ride on the backs of our book readers.[356]

356. [For this reason] we should meet the book needs, including popular books, of our readers before we strive to serve other people.[357]

357. Readers of popular books have a right to expect at least as good service as the readers of "unpopular" (scholarly, serious, etc.) books.[358]

358. Because of the easy accessibility of a vast number of books I draw the conclusion, perhaps un warranted, that almost all of American voluntary readers were "created" in public libraries.[359]

359. Many librarians seem diffident about what libraries do best (and what most people use libraries for).[360]

360. The most important factor, even more important than a pleasant staff, is the reasonable availability of wanted books at the time of their popularity.[361]

361. There are no public relations that can equal a reader finding a wanted book on the shelf. [362]

362. Timely availability of wanted books should be our watch words.[363]

363. One area where libraries may be better than bookstores, from the customer's point of view, is the provision of previously published books.[364]

364. By asking that books be read only for the sheer joy of reading, public libraries are major "creators" of America's avid readers.[365]

365. Readers, like me, who read reviews and try to find some of the books on the shelf have a better chance of winning the lottery.[366]

366. The first purpose of a library is to have books readers want to read within a reasonable period of time.[367]

367. As important as information is, most public library users use libraries for books and reading.[368]

368. The public library plays a major, but unrecognized, role in the creation and nurturing of America's good readers.[369]

369. In my view only book readers can be truly informed and only users of good libraries can get the full details because libraries keep books that go out of print.[370]

370. A major role of public libraries is hardly ever mentioned. Public libraries (along with families) may be a major creator and nurturer of America's voluntary readers.[371]

371. Timely availability of wanted books and other popular materials is the key to adult public library service.[372]

372. I believe the most used service of most public libraries, book lending, will become even more important because of the possible diminution of face-to-face reference service as more of the public get into the Internet.[373]

373. To the lay person having his/her desired books on the shelf is what libraries are for.[374]

374. The least expensive thing libraries do happens when a borrower finds a book (or "thing") on the shelf, borrows it, and returns it before overdue notices are generated.[375]

375. Readers should find something of interest every time they come to the library.[376]

376. Readers should have a feeling that the library is interested in their reading and that they can depend on the library.[377]

Reading

377. Reading may be the most efficient way of acquiring information.[378]

378. Even in this TV world, for ideas to take hold, books have to be read.[379]

379. Anyone who has sent for a TV or radio transcript knows, that reading, for most people, is usually a much faster way of gaining information than TV watching.[380]

380. Reading is a skill like basketball playing. Once you learn the basics the more you do the better you are at it.[381]

381. Lack of time was given as a major reasons for not reading, in a Book Industry Study Group study in the '70s. Message: don't mention *time* in reading related library messages.[382]

Reading Education

382. Schools, in their very effort to teach reading, may take the joy and pleasure out of reading.[383]

383. Schools, in the very act of teaching kids to read, and testing them to see if they actually have read the book assigned, wring much of the joy out of the joy of reading.[384]

384. I believe it's hard to learn to love reading with assigned reading coupled with book reports and exams.[385]

385. Schools may teach kids to read, but the "joy of reading" is usually learned at home or the public library.[386]

386. Schools usually cannot "teach" reading for pleasure because, in their desire to measure a student's progress, they couple reading with the "pain" of tests and book reports.[387]

387. The key to creating avid readers is uncoerced pleasurable reading.[388]

388. Let me take this opportunity to reiterate my view that public libraries, by inculcating the "Joy of Reading" in kids, are major generators of avid readers, people who enjoy reading so much, that they *voluntarily* buy newspapers, magazines, and books.[389]

389. Like learning another language, reading for pleasure is best "learned" early in life.[390]

390. Not only does reading to babies improve prospects for a brighter future; it is also an important factor in teaching a youngster to love reading. Every book read for pleasure hones one's skills, making reading even more pleasurable.[391]

391. Every book read for pleasure hones one's skills, making reading even more pleasurable.[392]

Reference Services

392. While studies have shown many people *need* information, I doubt that they *want* information.[393]

393. After thinking about it, I've decided "May I help you?" is a put-down. I try to use, "Are you finding what you want?" This involves both of us in the search. I also don't like, "I'll find it *for you*." It's our job. Just say, "I'll find it."[394]

Signage

394. One of the ways I instantly judge a library is by the neatness of their temporary signs.[395]
395. To me, signs are one public manifestation of a library's attitude toward its public. Sloppy signs usually mean, "all you can expect here is uncaring sloppy service."[396]

Weeding

396. In mature libraries, a book must be discarded for every one added.[397]
397. Inactivity is the prime consideration in weeding.[398]
398. The person who weeds should be the person who buys.[399]
399. "Collection" implies completeness and permanence, making it psychologically more difficult to weed.[400]
400. "Book stock" seems to be emotionally neutral, enabling us to more easily prune dead wood.[401]
401. "When in doubt, throw it out" is a good weeding slogan.[402]
402. It's far more difficult to weed than to buy. When buying, reviews, etc., are at hand. When weeding, the weeder is alone with his/her book knowledge.[403]
403. Even discards need appeal—if it's a dog in the library, it will be a dog out of the library.[404]

Notes

1. "Editor's Note," *U*L* no. 93 (1994): 6.
2. "Editor's Mumblings," *U*L* no. 24 (1977): 2.
3. "Editor's Mumblings," *U*L* no. 25 (1977): 2.
4. "Editor's Mumblings," *U*L* no. 21 (1976): 2.
5. "Editor's Note," *U*L* no. 38 (1981): 24.
6. "Editor's Note," *U*L* no. 73 (1989): 28.
7. "More Mumblings (Two Letters)," *U*L* no. 91 (1994): 7; "ALA Gets Practical," *Library Journal* 118, no. 15 (September 15, 1993): 8.
8. "Publishers' Subsidy," *U*L* no. 111 (1999): 15.
9. Regan Robinson,"Collection Wisdom from Marvin Scilken," *Librarians Collection Letter: A Monthly Newsletter for Collection Development Staff* 8, no. 9 (February 1999): 6.
10. "Editor's Note," *U*L* no. 102 (1997): 6.
11. Robinson, "Collection Wisdom from Marvin Scilken," 6.
12. "Editor's Mumblings," *U*L* no. 71 (1989): 2.
13. "Library Book Reviews: More Information Needed," *U*L* no. 73 (1989): 10.

14. Robinson, "Collection Wisdom from Marvin Scilken," 1.
15. "Editor's Mumblings," *U*L* no. 25 (1977): 2.
16. "Book Jacket Request Postcard," *U*L* no. 27 (1978): 13.
17. "Editor's Mumblings," *U*L* no. 50 (1984): 2.
18. "Editor's Mumblings," *U*L* no. 50 (1984): 2.
19. "Editor's Notes," *U*L* no. 61 (1986): 28.
20. "Editor's Note," *U*L* no. 102 (1997): 6.
21. Robinson, "Collection Wisdom from Marvin Scilken," 1.
22. "Editor's Note," *U*L* no. 40 (1981): 21.
23. "Libraries for an Age of Exploration (A Reader Interest Approach)," *U*L* no. 3 (Spring 1972): 26.
24. "Libraries for an Age of Exploration," 26.
25. "Libraries for an Age of Exploration," 27.
26. "Editor's Mumblings," *U*L* no. 48 (1983): 2.
27. "Editor's Note," *U*L* no. 58 (1986): 22.
28. "Editor's Mumblings," *U*L* no. 70 (1989): 2.
29. "Catchwords, Subtitles, and Synthetic Subtitles," *U*L* no. 1 (November 1971): 32.
30. "The Civil Service Test Book Problem (or Turning Turner Out)," *U*L* no. 1 (November 1971): 14.
31. "Lost in (Catalog) Space." *U*L* no. 3 (Spring 1972): 3.
32. "ISBD(M) Arrives," *U*L* no. 13 (Fall 1974): 16.
33. "Editor's Notes," *U*L* no. 14 (Winter 1975): 2.
34. "Manage Time: Do It Now!" *U*L* no. 28 (1978): 19.
35. "Editor's Note," *U*L* no. 40 (1981): 10.
36. "./=/[s.l.]s.n.]s.l.:s.n.] circa p.300 ill. [et.al.]," *U*L* no. 6 (Winter 1973): 21.
37. "./=/[s.l.]s.n.]s.l.:s.n.]," 21.
38. "Editor's Notes," *U*L* no. 14 (Winter 1975): 2.
39. "Editor's Notes and Ramblings," *U*L* no. 15 (Spring 1975): 3.
40. "Editor's Notes and Ramblings," *U*L* no. 15 (Spring 1975): 3.
41. "N.t.," *U*L* no. 46 (1983): 28.
42. "Editor's Note, *U*L* no. 32 (1979): 4.
43. "Editor's Mumblings," *U*L* no. 37 (1980): 2.
44. "Editor's Mumblings, *U*L* no. 37 (1980): 2.
45. "Editor's Mumblings, *U*L* no. 37 (1980): 2.
46. "Editor's Note," *U*L* no. 37 (1980): 7.
47. Joseph Deitch, "Portrait: Marvin Scilken," *Wilson Library Bulletin* 59, no. 3 (November 1984): 206.
48. "Editor's Mumblings," *U*L* no. 70 (1989): 2.
49. "Editor's Mumblings," *U*L* no. 70 (1989): 2.
50. "Classify to 'Merchandise,'" *U*L* no. 79 (1991): 11.
51. "Classify to 'Merchandise,'" 11.
52. "The Cover," *U*L* no. 108 (1998): 2.
53. "The Cover," *U*L* no. 108 (1998): 2.
54. "Manage Time: Do It Now!" *U*L* 28 (1978): 19.
55. "Editor's Mumblings," *U*L* no. 76 (1990): 2.
56. "Editor's Mumblings," *U*L* no. 24 (1977): 2.
57. "Editor's Notes and Ramblings," *U*L* no. 15 (Spring 1975): 3.
58. "Editor's Note," *U*L* no. 50 (1984): 18.

59. "Editor's Mumblings: *Libraries Should Focus on Books, Reading, and Literacy*," *U*L* no. 80 (1991): 2.
60. "Editor's Mumblings," *U*L* no. 41 (1981): 2.
61. "Editor's Mumblings," *U*L* no. 41 (1981): 2.
62. "Editor's Note," *U*L* no. 39 (1981): 4.
63. "Editor's Note," *U*L* no. 39 (1981): 4.
64. Editor's Note," *U*L* no. 57 (1985): 14.
65. "Editor's Mumblings: *Libraries Should Focus on Books, Reading, and Literacy*," 2.
66. "Libraries for an Age of Exploration," 26.
67. "Editor's Note, *U*L* no. 32 (1979): 4.
68. Deitch, "Portrait: Marvin Scilken," 207.
69. "Editor's Mumblings," *U*L* no. 62 (1987): 2.
70. "The Cover and Editor's Mumblings," *U*L*, no. 63 (1987): 2.
71. "Editor's Mumblings,"*U*L* no. 66 (1988): 2.
72. "Editor's Note," *U*L* no. 77 (1990): 17.
73. "Editor's Mumblings: *Libraries Should Focus on Books, Reading, and Literacy*," 2.
74. "Editor's Mumblings: *Libraries Should Focus on Books, Reading, and Literacy*," 2.
75. "ALA Candidates on ACRL," 244.
76. "ALA Candidates on ACRL," 244.
77. "The Library as Main Street's Ally," *New York Times*, 14 November 1993, 11(3).
78. "Editor's Mumblings," *U*L* no. 89 (1993): 2.
79. "Editor's Mumblings," *U*L* no. 102 (1997): 3.
80. "Editor's Note," *U*L* no. 107 (1998): 26.
81. "Editor's Note," *U*L* no. 107 (1998): 30.
82. "Editor's Mumblings," *U*L* no. 108 (1998): 3.
83. "Editor's Mumblings," *U*L* no. 109 (1998): 3.
84. "Editor's Mumblings," *U*L* no. 109 (1998): 3.
85. "Philosophy," *U*L* no. 113 (1999): 2.
86. "Editor's Notes," *U*L* no. 10 (Winter 1971): 2.
87. "Editor's Note," *U*L* no. 88 (1993): 31.
88. "Editor's Mumblings," *U*L* no. 39 (1971): 2.
89. "Rental Collection Pays Off," *U*L* no. 35 (1980): 15.
90. "Editor's Mumblings," *U*L* no. 39 (1981): 2.
91. "The Cover," *U*L* no. 47 (1982): 2.
92. "The Cover," *U*L* no. 47 (1982): 2.
93. "The Cover," *U*L* no. 47 (1982): 2.
94. "The Cover," *U*L* no. 47 (1982): 2.
95. "Cover," *U*L* no. 48 (1983): 1.
96. "Editor's Note," *U*L* no. 55 (1985): 20.
97. "Editor's Mumblings," *U*L* no. 71 (1989): 2.
98. "Editor's Mumblings," *U*L* no. 76 (1990): 2.
99. "Editor's Note," *U*L* no. 78 (1991): 3.
100. "Editor's Notes," *U*L* no. 106 (1998): 2.
101. "Editor's Notes," *U*L* no. 106 (1998): 2.
102. "Editor's Notes," *U*L* no. 106 (1998): 2.
103. "Retrieving Overdues—Some Thoughts," *U*L* no. 107 (1998): 2.

104. "Retrieving Overdues—Some Thoughts," 2.
105. "Retrieving Overdues—Some Thoughts," 2.
106. "Retrieving Overdues—Some Thoughts," 5.
107. Robinson, "Collection Wisdom from Marvin Scilken," 6.
108. Robinson, "Collection Wisdom from Marvin Scilken," 6.
109. "Editor's Mumblings," *U*L* no. 23 (1977): 2.
110. "Mumblings," *U*L* no. 27 (1978): 2.
111. "Letter to New Jersey Governor Brendan Byrne," *U*L* no. 28 (1978): 17.
112. "Some Arguments for Public Library Funding in an Urban Area," *U*L* no. 30 (1979): 28.
113. "The Cover," *U*L* no. 32 (1979): 2.
114. "Editor's Mumblings," *U*L* no. 47 (1983): 2.
115. "Editor's Note," *U*L* no. 53 (1984): 20.
116. "Editor's Notes," *U*L* no. 59 (1986): 29.
117. "Editor's Mumblings," *U*L* no. 82 (1992): 2.
118. "Editor's Note," *U*L* no. 86 (1993): 22.
119. "The Library as Main Street's Ally," 11(3).
120. "Editor's Note," *U*L* no. 92 (1994): 6.
121. "A Letter to *Harper's Magazine* on 'Silence, Please: The Public Library as Entertainment Center,'" *U*L* no. 101 (1996): 15.
122. "A Letter to *Harper's Magazine*," 15.
123. "A Letter to *Harper's Magazine*," 15.
124. "Editor's Mumblings," *U*L* no. 29 (1978): 2.
125. "Let's Put Some Realism in Public Library Public Relations," *U*L* no. 30 (1979): 11.
126. "Editor's Mumblings," *U*L* no. 76 (1990): 2.
127. "Some Random, Rambling Thoughts on Judge Sarokin's Decision," *U*L* no. 79 (1991): 17.
128. "Editor's Mumblings," *U*L* no. 85 (1992): 2.
129. "Editor's Note," *U*L* no. 85 (1992): 20.
130. "Indiana's Public Library Access Card (PLAC) Program (Statewide Library Card Program)," *U*L* no. 86 (1993): 23.
131. "Editor's Mumblings," *U*L* no. 89 (1993): 2.
132. "Editor's Mumblings," *U*L* no. 89 (1993): 2.
133. "The Library as Main Street's Ally," 11(3).
134. "More Mumblings: Public Library Funding," *U*L* no. 90 (1994): 3
135. "More Mumblings: Public Library Funding," 3.
136. "More Mumblings: Public Library Funding," 3.
137. "More Mumblings: Public Library Funding," 3.
138. "More Mumblings: Public Library Funding," 4.
139. "Editor's Note," *U*L* no. 93 (1994): 10.
140. "Editor's Mumblings," *U*L* no. 100 (1996): 2.
141. "Better Libraries," *U*L* no. 100 (1996): 8.
142. "Editor's Mumblings," *U*L* no. 101 (1996): 3.
143. "Note," *U*L* no. 104 (1997): 5.
144. "Editor's Mumblings," *U*L* no. 105 (1997): 3.
145. "Editor's Note," *U*L* no. 107 (1998): 25.
146. "Editor's Note," *U*L* no. 107 (1998): 25.
147. "Editor's Note," *U*L* no. 107 (1998): 26.
148. "Editor's Mumblings," *U*L* no. 109 (1998): 3.

149. "More Mumblings (Two Letters)," 7; "ALA Gets Practical," 10.

150. "Editor's Mumblings," *U*L* no. 23 (1977): 2.

151. "Some Arguments for Public Library Funding in an Urban Area," 28.

152. "Editor's Note," *U*L* no. 31 (1979): 3.

153. "Editor's Note." *U*L* no. 31 (1979): 3.

154. "Editor's Note." *U*L* no. 31 (1979): 3.

155. "*U*L* Offers," *U*L* no. 38 (1981): 32.

156. "[Look Smart Bumper Sticker]," New York: *U*L*, 1981.

157. "Thought for This Issue," *U*L* no. 64 (1987): 15.

158. "[Cover]," *U*L* no. 84 (1992): 1.

159. "[Cover]," *U*L* no. 84 (1992): 1.

160. "[Cover]," *U*L* no. 84 (1992): 1.

161. "Letter to a Legislator," *U*L* no. 87 (1993): 26.

162. "Editor's Mumblings," *U*L* no. 95 (1995): 2.

163. "Two Sentences That Public Librarians Should Include in Every Not-For-Publication Letter to a Print Editor," *U*L* no. 97 (1995): 4.

164. "The Original Letter to the *New York Times*," *U*L* no. 105 (1997): 10.

165. "Editor's Mumblings," *U*L* no. 109 (1998): 3.

166. "The Cover," *U*L* no. 33 (1979): 1.

167. "Editor's Note," *U*L* no. 67 (1988): 14.

168. "Indiana's Public Library Access Card," 23.

169. "Indiana's Public Library Access Card," 23.

170. "Library Postal Increase," *New York Times*, 5 January 1995, 26(A).

171. Deitch, "Portrait: Marvin Scilken," 206.

172. "Editor's Mumblings," *U*L* no. 89 (1993): 2.

173. "Editor's Mumblings," *U*L* no. 92 (1994): 2.

174. "Editor's Mumblings," *U*L* no. 23 (1977): 2.

175. "Editor's Mumblings," *U*L* no. 24 (1977): 2.

176. "Mumblings," *U*L* no. 27 (1978): 2.

177. "Mumblings," *U*L* no. 27 (1978): 2.

178. "Editor's Mumblings," *U*L* 28 (1978): 2.

179. "Let's Put Some Realism," 11.

180. "Editor's Mumblings," *U*L* no. 42 (1982): 2.

181. "Editor's Note," *U*L* no. 43 (1982): 13.

182. "The Cover and Mumblings," *U*L* no. 45 (1982): 2.

183. Deitch, "Portrait: Marvin Scilken," 207.

184. "Editor's Mumblings," *U*L* no. 54 (1985): 2.

185. "Editor's Note," *U*L* no. 55 (1985): 19.

186. "Editor's Note," *U*L* no. 55 (1985): 20.

187. "Editor's Comment," *U*L* no. 66 (1988): 9.

188. "Editor's Note," *U*L* no. 69 (1988): 12.

189. "Editor's Mumblings," *U*L* no. 76 (1990): 2.

190. "Editor's Mumblings," *U*L* no. 79 (1991): 2.

191. "Editor's Note," *U*L* no. 79 (1991): 4.

192. "Editor's Mumblings: *Libraries Should Focus on Books, Reading, and Literacy*," 2.

193. "Editor's Mumblings," *U*L* no. 81 (1992): 2.

194. "The Cover," *U*L* no. 83 (1992): 2.

195. "Front and Back Covers," *U*L* no. 84 (1992): 2.

196. "Editor's Mumblings," *U*L* no. 90 (1994): 2.

197. "Editor's Mumblings," *U*L* no. 90 (1994): 2.
198. "More Mumblings: Public Library Funding," *U*L* no. 90 (1994): 4.
199. "Editor's Mumblings," *U*L* no. 91 (1994): 2.
200. "Attendance Comparisons May Help Libraries," *U*L* no. 91 (1994): 4.
201. "More Mumblings (Two Letters)," 7; "ALA Gets Practical," 8.
202. "More Mumblings (Two Letters)," 7; "ALA Gets Practical," 8.
203. "More Mumblings (Two Letters)," 7; "ALA Gets Practical," 8.
204. "Editor's Mumblings," *U*L* no. 92 (1994): 2.
205. "Dear Editor," *U*L* no. 98 (1996): 22.
206. "Editor's Mumblings," no. *U*L* 100 (1996): 2.
207. "Editor's Mumblings," no. *U*L* 100 (1996): 2.
208. "Editor's Mumblings," no. *U*L* 102 (1997): 3.
209. "Library-Boosting Letters Rewarded," *U*L* 102 (1997): 4.
210. "Editor's Note," no. *U*L* 102 (1997): 28.
211. "More Mumblings: A Response to an Editorial in *Public Libraries*," *U*L* 103 (1997): 12.
212. "Editor's Mumblings," *U*L* no. 105 (1997): 3.
213. "Letter to Anthony Lewis," *U*L* no. 105 (1997): 8.
214. "Write On," *U*L* no. 107 (1998): 12.
215. "Editor's Note," *U*L* no. 107 (1998): 25.
216. "Editor's Mumblings," *U*L* no. 108 (1998): 3.
217. "Editor's Mumblings," *U*L* no. 108 (1998): 3.
218. "Editor's Mumblings," *U*L* no. 109 (1998): 3.
219. "Editor's Note," *U*L* no. 110 (1999): 25.
220. "A Visit to Brooklyn's Brighton Beach Branch," *U*L* no. 110 (1999): 26.
221. "Editor's Note," *U*L*, no. 112 (1999): 27.
222. "Editor's Mumblings," *U*L* no. 94 (1995): 2.
223. "Editor's Notes," *U*L* no. 11 (Spring 1974): 2.
224. "Editor's Notes," *U*L* no. 14 (Winter 1975): 2.
225. "The Cover," *U*L* no. 33 (1979): 1.
226. "Editor's Note," *U*L* no. 44 (1982): 6.
227. "Editor's Note," *U*L* no. 44 (1982): 6.
228. "Editor's Mumblings," *U*L* no. 75 (1990): 2.
229. "Editor's Mumblings," no. 77 (1990): 2.
230. "Editor's Note," *U*L* no. 77 (1990): 18.
231. "Libraries and Cooking," *New York Times*, 26 February 1992, 8(C).
232. "College Students in the Public Library: A Letter to the Editor of *New Jersey Libraries*," *U*L* no. 87 (1993): 2.
233. "More Mumblings: Public Library Funding," *U*L* no. 90 (1994): 4.
234. "Editor's Mumblings," *U*L* no. 102 (1997): 3.
235. "Editor's Note," *U*L* no. 107 (1998): 25.
236. "Philosophy," 2.
237. "Editor's Note," *U*L* no. 39 (1981): 16.
238. "Editor's Mumblings," *U*L* no. 58 (1986): 2.
239. "Editor's Mumblings," *U*L* no. 62 (1987): 2.
240. "The Cover and Editor's Mumblings," *U*L* no. 63 (1987): 2.
241. "The Cover and Editor's Mumblings," *U*L* no. 63 (1987): 2.
242. "Editor's Mumblings," *U*L* no. 73 (1989): 2.
243. "A Letter Written to Principals," *U*L* no. 84 (1992): 31.
244. "A Letter Written to Principals," 31.

245. "Discouraging 'T' Card Switching," *U*L* no. 8 (Summer 1973): 17.
246. "Editor's Note," *U*L* no. 35 (1980): 10.
247. "Editor's Note," *U*L* no. 35 (1980): 10.
248. "Coping with a Popular Record Collection," *U*L* no. 18 (Winter 1976): 31.
249. "Let's Put Some Realism," 11.
250. "Let's Put Some Realism," 11.
251. "The Cover," *U*L* no. 32 (1979): 2.
252. "Editor's Mumblings," *U*L* no. 42 (1982): 2.
253. "Editor's Mumblings," *U*L* no. 42 (1982): 2.
254. "Editor's Mumblings," *U*L* no. 42 (1982): 2.
255. "Do You Know, Can You Guess?" *U*L* no. 42 (1982): 8.
256. "The Cover," *U*L* no. 43 (1982): 2.
257. "The Cover," *U*L* no. 43 (1982): 2.
258. Deitch, "Portrait: Marvin Scilken," 207
259. Deitch, "Portrait: Marvin Scilken," 207.
260. "Editor's Mumblings," *U*L* no. 62 (1987): 2.
261. "Editor's Comments," *U*L* no. 71 (1989): 8.
262. "Editor's Mumblings,"*U*L* no. 72 (1989): 2.
263. "Editor's Mumblings," *U*L* no. 72 (1989): 2.
264. "The Cover: Library Users and Voting," *U*L* no. 77 (1990): 3.
265. "The Cover: Library Users and Voting," 3.
266. "College Students in the Public Library," 2.
267. "Editor's Notes," *U*L* no. 87 (1993): 24.
268. "Letter to a Legislator," 26.
269. "To The Editor of *Public Libraries*," *U*L* no. 91 (1994): 7.
270. "Editor's Mumblings," *U*L* no. 97 (1995): 2.
271. "Editor's Notes," *U*L* no. 106 (1998): 2.
272. Robinson, "Collection Wisdom from Marvin Scilken," 6.
273. "A Note," *U*L* no. 1 (November 1971): 2.
274. "A Note," *U*L* no. 1 (November 1971): 2.
275. "Editor's Notes," *U*L* no. 5 (Fall 1972): 1.
276. "Super Card Notes from the Editor," *U*L* no. 15 (Spring 1975): 13.
277. "Editor's Mumblings," *U*L* no. 21 (1976): 2.
278. "Editor's Mumblings," *U*L* no. 24 (1977): 2.
279. "Editor's Mumblings," *U*L* no. 24 (1977): 2.
280. "Mumblings," *U*L* no. 27 (1978): 2.
281. "Editor's Mumblings," *U*L* no. 29 (1978): 2.
282. "The Cover," *U*L* no. 33 (1979): 1.
283. "Editor's Note," *U*L* no. 42 (1982): 4.
284. "Editor's Note," *U*L* no. 44 (1982): 7.
285. "Editor's Note," *U*L* no. 72 (1989): 10.
286. "Editor's Notes," *U*L* no. 101 (1996): 20.
287. "Backlog to Frontlog: A Scheme for Circulating Nonfiction Books Without the Help of the Library of Congress," *Library Journal* 94 (16) (September 15, 1969): 3015.
288. "Publishers' 'Net Price' Library Editions," *U*L* no. 6 (Winter 1973): 32.
289. "The Read and Return Collection: A Scheme for Overcoming Librarians' Reluctance to Buy Multiple Copies of Popular Books," *Wilson Library Bulletin* 46, no. 1 (September 1971): 104; *U*L* no. 7 (Spring 1973): 12.
290. "The Read and Return Collection," 12.

291. "The Read and Return Collection," 12.
292. "The Read and Return Collection," 12.
293. "Editor's Note," *U*L* no. 25 (1977): 26.
294. "Random Selection of Stocks and Books," *U*L* no. 28 (1978): 8.
295. "Editor's Note," *U*L* no. 38 (1981): 7.
296. "Editor's Mumblings," *U*L* no. 39 (1981): 2.
297. "'Stock'ing Books," *U*L* no. 41 (1981): 32.
298. Deitch, "Portrait: Marvin Scilken," 206.
299. "Suggestions to Library Book Reviewing Journals," *U*L* no. 51 (1984): 32.
300. "Editor's Note," *U*L* no. 55 (1985): 20.
301. "Editor's Note," *U*L* no. 55 (1985): 20.
302. "Editor's Mumblings," no. 71 (1989): 2.
303. "Editor's Mumblings," *U*L* no. 71 (1989): 2.
304. "Library Book Reviews," 10.
305. "Editor's Mumblings," *U*L* no. 76 (1990): 2.
306. "Recommended Author on the Middle East," *U*L* no. 76 (1990): 14.
307. "Editor's Mumblings," *U*L* no. 83 (1992): 2.
308. "Editor's Note,'" *U*L* no. 90 (1994): 7.
309. "Letter on HarperCollins Book Discounts," *U*L* no. 101 (1996): 21.
310. "Letter on HarperCollins Book Discounts," 21.
311. Robinson, "Collection Wisdom from Marvin Scilken," 6.
312. "Editor's Note," *U*L* no. 35 (1980): 21.
313. "Editor's note, *U*L* no. 39 (1981): 4.
314. "Editor's Note," *U*L* no. 69 (1988): 12.
315. "Editor's Note," *U*L* no. 69 (1988): 12.
316. "The Cover," *U*L* no. 86 (1993): 2.
317. "The Cover," *U*L* no. 86 (1993): 2.
318. "Editor's Note," *U*L* no. 93 (1994): 10.
319. "Editor's Mumblings," *U*L* no. 107 (1998): 3.
320. "Editor's Mumblings," *U*L* no. 107 (1998): 3.
321. "Unpublished Letter to the *Times*," *U*L* no. 15 (Spring 1975): 13.
322. "Editor's Note," *U*L* no. 35 (1980): 6.
323. "Editor's Note," *U*L* no. 35 (1980): 6.
324. "Editor's Note," *U*L* no. 38 (1981): 24.
325. "Editor's Mumblings," *U*L* no. 44 (1982): 2.
326. "Editor's Mumblings," *U*L* no. 49 (1983): 2.
327. Deitch, "Portrait: Marvin Scilken," 207.
328. "Editor's Note," *U*L* no. 55 (1985): 19.
329. "Editor's Notes," *U*L* no. 61 (1986): 28.
330. "Editor's Mumblings," *U*L* no. 74 (1990): 2.
331. "Editor's Mumblings," *U*L* no. 74 (1990): 2.
332. "[Letter to James P. Schadt]," *U*L* no. 91 (1994): 5.
333. "Dear Editor," *U*L* no. 98 (1996): 22.
334. "Editor's Mumblings," *U*L* no. 34 (1980): 2.
335. "Editor's Mumblings," *U*L* no. 41 (1981): 2.
336. "Editor's Mumblings," *U*L* no. 41 (1981): 2.
337. "Editor's Note," *U*L* no. 57 (1985): 30.
338. "The Cover," *U*L* no. 75 (1990): 2.
339. "The Cover," *U*L* no. 75 (1990): 2.
340. "Editor's Mumblings," *U*L* no. 87 (1993): 2.

341. "Postscript," *U*L* no. 7 (Spring 1973): 13.

342. "CIP vs. COP," *U*L* no. 10 (Winter 1974): 31.

343. "Editor's Notes and Ramblings," *U*L* no. 15 (Spring 1975): 3.

344. "Editor's Mumblings," *U*L* no. 32 (1979): 2.

345. "Rental Collection Pays Off," *U*L* no. 35 (1980): 15.

346. "Editor's Note," *U*L* no. 39 (1981): 16.

347. "Editor's Mumblings," *U*L* no. 47 (1983): 2.

348. "Editor's Mumblings," *U*L* no. 47 (1983): 2.

349. "The Cover," *U*L* no. 50 (1984): 2.

350. Deitch, "Portrait: Marvin Scilken," 207.

351. "Rotarian Librarian," *The Rotarian* 144 (June 1984): 47.

352. "Editor's Note," *U*L* no. 55 (1985): 19.

353. "Editor's Note," *U*L* no. 64 (1987): 5.

354. "Editor's Note," *U*L* no. 71 (1989): 18.

355. "Editor's Mumblings," *U*L* no. 75 (1990): 2.

356. "Editor's Mumblings," *U*L* no. 76 (1990): 2.

357. "Editor's Mumblings," *U*L* no. 76 (1990): 2.

358. "Editor's Mumblings," *U*L* no. 76 (1990): 2.

359. "Editor's Mumblings: *Libraries Should Focus on Books, Reading, and Literacy*," 2.

360. "Editor's Mumblings: *Libraries Should Focus on Books, Reading, and Literacy*," 2.

361. "Editor's Mumblings," *U*L* no. 83 (1992): 2.

362. "Editor's Mumblings," *U*L* no. 83 (1992): 2.

363. "Editor's Mumblings," *U*L* no. 83 (1992): 2.

364. "'Sell More of What Sells'—Backlist Books," *U*L* no. 84 (1992): 14.

365. "Reading for Pleasure, Not Just for Tests," *New York Times*, 4 October 1992, 16(4).

366. "Editor's Mumblings," *U*L* no. 87 (1993): 2.

367. "Libraries," *New York Times*, 27 June 1993, 10(10).

368. John N. Berry III, "ALA's Agenda: Let's Get On with it," *Library Journal* 118, no. 12 (July 1993): 6.

369. "[Letter to James P. Schadt]," 5.

370. "Editor's Mumblings," *U*L* no. 96 (1995): 2.

371. "A Letter to *Harper's Magazine*," 15.

372. "Editor's Note," *U*L* no. 103 (1997): 12.

373. "Editor's Mumblings," *U*L* no. 104 (1997): 3.

374. "Editor's Note," *U*L* no. 107 (1998): 30.

375. "Editor's Note," *U*L* no. 107 (1998): 30.

376. Robinson, "Collection Wisdom from Marvin Scilken," 1.

377. Robinson, "Collection Wisdom from Marvin Scilken," 6.

378. "In Case You Never Thought About It," *U*L* no. 69 (1988): 6.

379. "Letter Written to Paul E. Tsongas, Presidential Candidate," *U*L* no. 79 (1991): 4.

380. "The Cover," *U*L* no. 102 (1997): 2,

381. "The Basketball Court of Reading," *U*L* no. 103 (1997): 18,

382. "Editor's Note," *U*L* no. 110, 1999, 18.

383. "The Cover and Editor's Mumblings,"*U*L* no. 57 (1985): 2.

384. "Editor's Note," *U*L* no. 70 (1989): 18.

385. Editor's Mumblings: *Libraries Should Focus on Books, Reading, and Literacy*," 2.
386. "[Letter to James P. Schadt]," 4.
387. "[Letter to James P. Schadt]," 5.
388. "Reading for Pleasure," 16(4).
389. "Two Sentences That Public Librarians Should Include," 4.
390. "A Letter to *Harper's Magazine*," 15.
391. "Brain Food for Babies," *Time* 149, no. 8 (February 24, 1997): 10.
392. "Brain Food for Babies," 10.
393. "Editor's Mumblings," *U*L* no. 34 (1980): 2.
394. "Editor's Note," *U*L* no. 96 (1995): 31.
395. "Editor's Mumblings," *U*L* no. 108 (1998): 3.
396. "Editor's Mumblings: Temporary Signs," *U*L* no. 108 (1998): 3.
397. "Some Thoughts on Weeding," *U*L* no. 1 (November 1971): 24.
398. "Some Thoughts on Weeding," 24.
399. "[Editor's Note]," *U*L* no. 36 (1980): 31.
400. "Editor's Mumblings," *U*L* no. 71 (1989): 2.
401. "Editor's Mumblings," 2.
402. "Editor's Mumblings," 2.
403. "Editor's Note," *U*L* no. 78 (1991): 3.
404. Deitch, "Portrait: Marvin Scilken," 205.

Chapter 8

Marvin H. Scilken's Statement for Council Candidacy

Marvin H. Scilken, editor and publisher, the *U*N*A*B*A*S*H*E*D Librarian, The 'How I Run My Library Good' Letter*, G.P.O. Box 2631, New York, NY 10116: November 1971.

EDUCATION

University of Colorado-Boulder, BA, 1948; Pratt Institute, MLS, 1960.

AMERICAN LIBRARY ASSOCIATION ACTIVITIES

Four terms on Council. Candidate for ALA President. Served on various committees. President, Junior Members' Round Table (now New Members Round Table).

STATE, REGIONAL LIBRARY, AND OTHER ASSOCIATION ACTIVITIES

Executive Board of New Jersey Library Association (NJLA). Served on various committees.

HONORS AND AWARDS

Mayor's Martin Luther King Human Rights Award, 1990. Pratt Institute
Alumnus of the Year, 1995. Beta Phi Mu member.

ACCOMPLISHMENTS

1. 1963–1993. Hands-on, front-line Library Director of Orange (New Jersey)
Public Library. Selected most adult titles. Cataloged for fifteen years.
Developed the "Frontlog"system to make "just arrived" books immediately
browsable and available to readers. Developed the "Read and Return
Collection," bringing surplus books to readers throughout the city.
2. In 1971 started (and continue to publish) the *U*N*A*B*A*S*H*E*D
Librarian, The 'How I Run My Library Good' Letter*, to provide a forum for
practical, innovative ideas, library humor, etc.
3. In 1992 was instrumental in getting Bell Atlantic to continue giving out-
of-town telephone directories to public libraries in Maryland, Virginia, D.C.,
New Jersey, West Virginia, and Pennsylvania. It is estimated that this will
save libraries from $350,000 to $750,000 a year.
4. Inveterate letter writer and library booster and advocate.
5. "Library letters" have appeared in the *New York Times, Time, Newsweek,
Business Week, Wall Street Journal, Spy, New York, New Jersey Monthly,
Newark Star-Ledger*, etc.
6. At my suggestion NJLA established awards to reward media people for
good library stories.
7. In 1966 called to the attention of, and testified before, the U.S. Senate
Subcommittee on Antitrust and Monopoly about the alleged price-fixing of
library books. As a result of the hearings some one thousand suits were
filed. Libraries (and their lawyers) recovered over $10 million of the $54
million in over-charges (perhaps $300 million in today's dollars). ALA
played no role in this.
8. Introduced in ALA Council a successful resolution that caused two of the
three major library wholesalers to compute libraries' discounts on the lower
"invoice price" rather than the higher jacket (Freight Passthrough) price.
9. Introduced in ALA Council a successful resolution that requested book
publishers to give libraries discounts equal to booksellers for equal-size
orders. ALA management ignored this Council resolution.
10. I have spoken at many conferences and workshops and contributed
articles and letters to professional publications.
11. Caused Council to reconsider bestowing ALA's highest award, Honorary
Membership, to a person who pleaded the publishers' case at the U.S. Senate
hearings.
12. I have been called the library world's Ralph Nader. If elected, I will
continue to work for the library users and the taxpaying public.

ALA MEMBER SINCE 1959

STATEMENT OF PROFESSIONAL CONCERNS

As important as information is, most adult public library users use libraries for books and reading. One of the most important roles of libraries, therefore, is the provision of books that readers want to read *when* they want to read them (good customer service). I view American society as an inverted pyramid. We all depend on the thoughtfulness of informed *readers* at the apex.

On Council I will work to:

1. Raise the visibility and status of libraries and librarians (the recent Benton Report found most Americans believe we could be replaced by bookstore clerks) in the American psyche and society. For instance, sponsoring a monthly column in the Sunday *New York Times*.

2. Get libraries recognition as the creator and nurturer of most of America's voluntary readers. Voluntary readers are the people who buy books, magazines, and newspapers.

3. Get libraries a fair shake for books and other things they buy.

Part III

Tributes and Biographies

Chapter 9

Marvin Scilken: A Personal and Professional Introduction

Mary P. ("Polly") Scilken

Marvin H. Scilken was born in New York City in 1926, the second child of immigrant parents, and lived in New York all his life. After receiving his diploma from the Bronx High School of Science, he attended the University of Colorado-Boulder, graduating in 1948.

After about ten years in a variety of positions in the business world, he responded to an ad in the *New York Times* announcing scholarships available for Library School. He was readily accepted into the master's of library science (MLS) program at Pratt Institute (Brooklyn, New York) and completed the program in 1960. He was certified by the New York State Department of Education as a "Public Librarian" in July of 1960. He took the diploma and certificate as license and admonition to proceed to advocacy for libraries and librarians. He held a series of librarian positions on Long Island (New York) and Westchester County (New York) before assuming directorship of the Orange (New Jersey) Public Library in 1963. He retired in 1993.

Marvin attended his first American Library Association (ALA) Annual meeting in Montreal in 1960. He was a quick study in the profession of librarianship. He quickly became a passionate advocate for libraries and librarians. He valued ALA and attended almost every annual meeting since he received his MLS. He served as President of Junior Members Round Table (now New Members Round Table), was elected to the ALA Council for five terms, but was defeated in his candidacy for ALA President. He was, in addition, active in New Jersey and New York City library organizations.

In 1966 Marvin testified before the U.S. Senate Antitrust and Monopoly Subcommittee, pointing out publishers' practices of price fixing books sold to libraries. In his formal statement before the subcommittee on March 22, 1966, he said, "Entering the library profession from the business world some six years ago, I was astounded by the fact that my library and other libraries were charged 'net prices' on some of the books purchased."[1] Outraged by his observation of pricing practices in the book industry, he successfully brought action on this issue by concertedly writing letters to a wide variety of persons. As a result of these hearings, schools and libraries filed over a thousand suits. They recovered some $10 million in overcharges. Over the course of his career, he continued to be surprised by the nonbusiness approach to library management by many librarians. When visiting other libraries, he often asked the staff how the library was supported. He was surprised that a large number didn't know the answer.

His effort to counter price fixing was just the beginning of a life-long aggressive campaign of letter writing and other activities on behalf of libraries and librarians. Whether he was traveling or at home, he was always on the alert for a link between published articles and relevant issues about literacy, reading, libraries, or librarians. He wrote letters to the *New York Times* and other major newspapers, *Time*, *Newsweek*, and *Business Week*. His letters were published in a wide variety of periodicals in addition to all the major library journals. Throughout his public library career he was passionate about library service and remained a dedicated advocate.

In 1971 Marvin began publishing the *U*N*A*B*A*S*H*E*D Librarian (U*L)*. This quarterly publication was designed to provide a forum in which librarians could share practical "how I run my library good" ideas. He was an innovative and user-oriented librarian and published many of his own ideas in the magazine. The *U*L* continues to be published.

Despite his untiring and unabashed professional efforts, Marvin always had time to be a wonderful husband, father, and grandfather.

Notes

1. Subcommittee on Antitrust and Monopoly of the Committee on the Judiciary, *Alleged Price Fixing of Library Books: Hearings on S. Res. 191*, 89th Congress, 2nd sess., 23 March 1966, 24 March 1966, and 12 May 1966, 16.

Chapter 10

Scilken, Marvin H. (1926–1999)

Dan O'Connor

Marvin Herman Scilken was born on December 7, 1926, in Bronx, New York, to Joseph Simon Scilken and Esther Berger Scilken.[1] His parents were born in separate parts of Russia and immigrated to the United States where they met and married. Marvin Scilken had an older sister, Marjorie, whom he kept in contact with throughout his life. He was a proud graduate of the 1945 class of the Bronx High School of Science in New York City. His bachelor's degree was in economics and philosophy from the University of Colorado-Boulder.

Scilken worked in the family's refrigeration business and for a marketing company, Pulse. He traveled widely in Europe, lived in Paris, and was particularly fond of the time he spent in Morocco where he worked at an air base. Upon return to the United States, Scilken, an inveterate reader, responded to a New York State notice in a newspaper offering scholarships to educate librarians. Upon learning that Columbia University's application deadline had passed, he entered and subsequently earned his Master of Library Science degree in 1960 from the Library School at Pratt Institute in Brooklyn, New York. Scilken's first library position was at Lindenhurst Public Library in Long Island.

In 1962 Scilken married Mary P. Martin, known as Polly. They had two sons, Jonathan and David. The family lived in mid-Manhattan, did not own an automobile, but would rent cars for well-planned vacations. Scilken treasured attending library conferences and felt that this was an essential means to learn of new developments while influencing others with his ideas. He was to eventually run for the Council of the American Library Association (ALA), where he served five consecutive terms. He amassed the highest vote count in Councilor elections while professing to run as an underdog. He often wore colorful Western clothing at national, state, and international conferences, which he attended with his wife. They valued the many friends they had in the library profession and they were well-known by thousands of librarians.

In 1963 Scilken became Director of the Orange Public Library in northern New Jersey, a city near Newark with a population of 35,789. He stayed in this position until he retired in 1993. The dynamic Scilken was well-known in Orange as a tireless advocate for the public library which was located in an impressive Greek revival building designed by Stanford White. The library contained architectural features unique to libraries, and Scilken was enthusiastic in pointing these out to visitors.

Scilken used this library as a base for his lifelong campaign to champion libraries and library services, especially reading. He undoubtedly drew from his earlier business and marketing experience the importance for vigorous promotion of the public library through constant use of slogans, letters to editors, and even awards to newspapers to keep all reminded of the importance of the role libraries have in our democratic society.

Scilken entered the library field as it was being pulled by two forces: development where support is garnered to create services for citizens, and efficiency where management techniques are used to improve internal operations to benefit library users. Scilken prided himself on making obvious a view of libraries from the perspective of the user and he offered persistent reminders that the public library belonged not to the librarians, but to the citizens whom he viewed as the real owners of the public library. This belief was manifest in his lifelong passion to promote reading, public library use, and efficient service to library users.

In the mid-1960s, Scilken made an early and important mark on the library field when he wrote a letter to New Jersey Senator Clifford Case that the net or no-discount book prices paid to publishers and wholesalers by public and school libraries was, in effect, subsidizing the discounts these same publishers offered to bookstores and others. Senator Case referred the letter to Senator Philip A. Hart, chair of the U.S. Senate's Subcommittee on Antitrust and Monopoly of the Committee of the Judiciary. Three days of hearings were held on "Alleged Price Fixing of Library Books" during the spring of 1966, with testimony and exhibits presented by librarians, publishers, book wholesalers, the American Book Publishers Council, and The Library Binding Institute. The subcommittee issued a report of 177 pages pursuant to offering a Senate Resolution. Price fixing was documented confirming Scilken's charge that prices charged libraries violated antitrust laws. Libraries entered into a series of suits to recover this money and Scilken's national reputation was established. *Wilson Library Bulletin* was to report in 1972 that libraries had entered into law suits to recover $10 million in rebates to resolve unfair pricing; later, other sources reported that over one thousand suits had been filed.

While Scilken prided himself on being a library consumer advocate, similar to Ralph Nader, he was perceived by many as being a gadfly who constantly attacked the library establishment. His causes were many and he pursued them vigorously and with flair. Drawing attention to an issue often meant that attention was focused on him. For example, he advocated allowing library users to read and circulate books acquired by the library which were in a backlog awaiting cataloging information from the Library of Congress. This system, heralded by Scilken as a Frontlog, was user focused but it contradicted long standing traditional library practice. Scilken drew attention to himself as he became a national advocate for this efficiency. He wrote a 1969 article on it for *Library Journal* and he had it mentioned in other features in the library press for a number of years. Yet, as much as it might appear self-serving to gain repeated publicity for this idea, Scilken consistently gave credit to Harry Dewey, his beloved professor at Pratt's Library School, who first thought of this efficiency. Scilken always gave credit to others for their ideas even while being criticized for directing the spotlight on himself.

In Scilken's early library career he was often misinterpreted as an individual seeking publicity. In point of fact, he sought to direct attention to the library user. He saw himself as an agent who served that user and he was quick and persistent in advancing any practice—developed by anyone—that improved the ultimate goal to provide books for library users. Important in his view was broadcasting practical ideas which improved public library service to users.

It was this motivation that inspired him to create his own publication, the *U*N*A*B*A*S*H*E*D Librarian, the "How I Run My Library Good" Letter*. The title's use of asterisks and its design came from his brother-in-law—a designer at Harper & Row, which had published Leo Rosten's 1937 novel, *The Education of H*Y*M*A*N K*A*P*L*A*N*. The subtitle is thought to come from library educators who proclaimed that they were *not* in the business of teaching graduate students "how I run my library good." The asterisks within the word U*N*A*B*A*S*H*E*D were effective in giving attention to Scilken's journal which was a potpourri of practical ideas, original and reprinted articles, humor and cartoons, and guides to cataloging practice and collection development—all focused on better service to library users.

Scilken, the iconoclast, took pride that he could provide practical professional information to a field that was quickly becoming overly theoretical and unnecessarily technological. Ever the pragmatist, he considered it entirely appropriate to encourage librarians to use postcards where they had previously prepared letters, to educate publishers about libraries and librarians, and, in all things, to view the world through a library lens.

Scilken's and his wife Polly compiled, edited, and published the *U*N*A*B*A*S*H*E*D Librarian* which, with its several thousand subscribers, produced important income for them to attend conferences, subscribe to pertinent publications, and keep abreast of developments in the library field. It also produced a profit that added to its remarkable success. After Marvin Scilken died, the publication was pursued by a number of individuals and was eventually purchased by Maurice Freedman, a long-term friend and colleague.

The influence of the *U*N*A*B*A*S*H*E*D Librarian* was remarkable because it was unlike other library publications and served primarily as a forum to share ideas and good practice. Further, it would often be located by library school students doing term papers who would quote it and later, as librarians, would rely on it for its strengths, especially its reprinting of effective public relations campaigns in the United States, Canada, and other countries. Relying on slogans, sound-bites, effective one line summaries of research, and even truisms gave the *U*N*A*B*A*S*H*E*D Librarian* a unique and memorable place in library literature. That it was criticized as not being scholarly or peer reviewed gave Scilken special satisfaction since he had stated in issue number one, November 1971, that it is an "informal *non-scholarly* letter for the exchange of useful ideas . . . [which] *may or may not be new.*"[2]

Early issues of the *U*N*A*B*A*S*H*E*D Librarian* gave attention to cataloging errors made by the Library of Congress (LC) and called for more efficient ways to help users find books. Scilken was proud that he was a proponent of more ideas than even he could implement at Orange Public Library. He was especially critical of the way books were classified by the Library of Congress and he often made suggestions to the Dewey Decimal catalogers at LC.

Later issues of the *U*N*A*B*A*S*H*E*D Librarian* focused on the importance of convincing the general public and elected officials that the library deserved their support. Scilken was one of the first to add questions to a general population survey asking voters about their library use. He spurred the New Jersey Library Association into giving the state's newspapers many special, annual awards for publishing library stories and these awards have grown in size and in stature since their inception. Scilken continued in his quest to save libraries money and was a driving force in making sure that the phone company serving the Mid-Atlantic states did not charge libraries for phone books—especially since the phone books used in libraries increased the use of the phone service. Scilken was also an effective advocate for the continuation of library postage rates and worked assiduously to develop positions to protect and defend differential postal charges favorable to libraries.

Scilken knew there was a thin line between irritation and producing action, and he was tireless in his persistence in promoting certain ideas. To sound out others, he telephoned colleagues to gather new ideas or defend an existing idea. These telephone calls added to his legend as a provocateur and even pesky advocate.

Scilken saw himself as a proponent of a serious library message to bring reading, especially by children, to the attention of the public. He wrote a steady series of short, memorable letters to the editors of major newspapers and library journals in an attempt to influence library thinking. Scilken was proud when these letters would be published, especially those printed by the *New York Times*. Even on vacation he would read local newspapers and send letters to them regarding libraries. He saw newspapers stories as often having a library component, that every story was potentially a library story giving him an opportunity to write to a newspaper or a politician. He had letters printed in *Texas Highways, American Way, Smithsonian, Newsweek,* and *Digital Time Magazine.* Further, he would often reprint published letters in the *U*N*A*B*A*S*H*E*D Librarian,* and, on occasion, would reprint a letter previously reprinted. He would regularly attack his local library, a branch of the New York Public Library for not stocking enough new books, but his motivation was clear in trying to get New York City to recognize the importance of its library system, which could provide so much to the citizens for a modest investment by the taxpayer.

At ALA Council meetings Scilken frequently got in line to make comments at the microphone. His incredible memory of past Council actions and library events made him a valuable voice in insuring that the organization did not contradict itself. In one case, ALA had earlier criticized an individual whom—years later—they proposed for an award. It was Scilken who reminded them of their earlier actions. Scilken also reminded ALA of its folly in obsessing on protracted issues unrelated to the users of libraries. In his early Council years, Scilken was sometimes identified as an independent and, at times, argumentative voice. In later years, he became valued by many as a friend and even as an institution within ALA—so much so that it worked to marginalize the message he was trying to convey. Scilken was serious about the issues he championed, but his good-natured manner often betrayed his intent and worked to reduce the impact he wanted to have. On the other hand, he talked in a deliberate manner to keep in check a speech impediment, and this worked effectively to have others listen more closely to the content of his messages.

Marvin Scilken, ever the critic and eventually the well-liked and respected colleague, was consistent in his message that libraries belonged to the citizens and that they were not institutions to employ librarians who had been educated at accredited graduate library programs. He tried to direct the attention of others to the good that libraries did for society and he framed a wider horizon from which to view libraries and librarians. Letters to editors, comments at microphones, endless phone calls and faxes were the methodologies he employed in communicating a message he knew was important to his field and to the average citizen, for whom he had the highest regard.

It was while he was attending an ALA Midwinter Conference that he died of an apparent heart attack on the evening of February 2, 1999. Scilken leaves behind an enviable record of accomplishments defined according to his terms viewed through the perspective of the library user. Pratt Institute named him Alumnus of the Year in 1994. His publication, the U*N*A*B*A*S*H*E*D *Librarian*, continues as a reminder of his goal and motto that informed his campaign when running for ALA President in 1991: "S*C*I*L*K*E*N: Working to Get Libraries the Credit They Deserve."

Notes

1. Donald G. Davis, Jr., ed. *Second Supplement to the Dictionary of American Library Biography* (Englewood, Colo.: Libraries Unlimited, in press), s.v. "Scilken, Marvin H. (1926–1999)."
2. Marvin Scilken, "A Note," *U*L* no. 1 (Nov. 1971): 2.

Chapter 11

Marvin's Legacy

Jack Forman

Marvin Scilken's sudden and tragic death during the 1999 American Library Association (ALA) Midwinter Meeting in Philadelphia leaves a gaping hole in librarianship.

I first laid eyes on his unassuming and widely-read publication, the *U*N*A*B*A*S*H*E*D Librarian*, when I began my library career in the Free Public Library of Woodbridge in 1968. From that first moment I knew that Marvin Scilken was special. He passionately, thoroughly, and unabashedly celebrated the world of librarianship by disseminating the folk wisdom of working librarians to colleagues all over the world.

Inspired by (and perhaps modeled on) Leo Rosten's humorous classic *THE EDUCATION OF H*Y*M*A*N K*A*P*L*A*N*, the *U*N*A*B*A*S*H*E*D Librarian* mirrors the spirit and message of Rosten's award-winning anecdotal stories about the acculturation of American immigrants to New York City in the 1930s.[1] The Jewish, Italian, German, and Russian characters of his book speak the colorful, funny, meaningful, and mangled language of the new immigrant. They were poor and lived in crowded tenements, but Rosten shows how their desire to become Americans and learn English overshadowed all else.

Hyman Kaplan was the quintessential immigrant. He spent most of his free time in adult education classes writing essays in massacred English. Kaplan's last essay in the novel says it all:

> Sometime I feel sad about how som people are living. Only sleeping eating working in shop. Not *thinking*. They are just like Enimals the same, which don't thinking also. Humans should not be like Enimals! They should *Thinking!* This is with me a deep idea. . . .

105

By *Thinking* is Humans making big edvences on Enimals. This we
call Progriss. . . .
ps. I dont care if I dont pass, I *love* the class."[2]

Who else but a devoted believer in democracy would edit and publish a
publication that consisted almost entirely of articles written by librarians in the
field—not by self-appointed leaders or authorities? Marvin believed that the
librarian rank and file could perform *tikkun olam* on librarianship—that they
could repair the world of librarianship so all of us could become better librarians.
Many of these librarians never wrote for publication before they wrote for the
*U*N*A*B*A*S*H*E*D Librarian*. Topics ranged across a broad spectrum of
interests: the joy (and importance) of cataloging; how to get along with a board
of trustees; all kinds of censorship problems, issues, and challenges; and the
planning and implementation of mainstream and off-beat library programs for all
age groups, some successful, some not. You never knew what you would find
imbedded in each issue—until you turned the page. His publication was a real
page-turner and very few who read the newsletter skipped a page.

I particularly remember the countless homegrown bibliographies and
booklists that Marvin published—lists that librarians put together with care and
love and tested with patrons. I learned from these articles. I was inspired by
them. And at the risk of being told to "get a life already," I confess that I often
lived vicariously through the experiences related in the articles.

I also remember Marvin's unabashed editorial contributions to his
publication. He was very modest about his own wisdom, which was
considerable. Articles he personally wrote for his publication often focused on the
need for better public relations, showing how librarians could make their services
and skills more visible to the public. Most of all I remember how he cajoled his
fellow librarians to write about their Fulghum-like professional experiences in
hopes they would teach valuable lessons to their colleagues.

Marvin's publication tried to repair the world of librarianship humorously,
never solemnly or preachingly, always optimistically. He wanted librarians to
think and act like humans. And Marvin didn't care if he got a high grade with
his newsletter—he just loved the class. "Progriss"—that's Marvin's legacy to us.

The *U*N*A*B*A*S*H*E*D Librarian* has been an editorial mentor to
hundreds of librarians. So it is not surprising that Marvin was my mentor on
ALA Council when I was first elected in 1987. I had been active in ALA
divisional activities for fifteen years, but all I knew about the ALA Council was
that it was big and complex. Marvin was assigned to be my mentor. He
generously treated me to lunch after the first Council meeting I attended. He
patiently answered my questions, demystified the Byzantine intricacies of the
Council, and introduced me to other Council members—mostly activists like
himself, from whom I took my cue. In typical self-deprecating modesty, Marvin
insistingly claimed I was *his* mentor, which, of course, is a joke. Any knowledge
I gained about Council and any energy I invested in being a Councilor I derived
from watching and listening to Marvin and his wide circle of friends.

We all miss Marvin, and I, in particular, do. I don't remember one meeting
in my seven years on Council when Marvin's voice was not raised on one issue
or another. Sometimes people rolled their eyes—not at what he was saying but

that Marvin was speaking yet again. But few failed to listen to him, especially when he spoke with reason, passion, and authority on issues important to him: wasteful spending in ALA, the public's right to information, the privacy of patron records, and, most recently, his courageous insistence that ALA membership meetings have a reasonable quorum requirement. He wanted to prevent future incidents where a small group of committed activists could dictate ALA policy in the name of ALA membership. And, of course, Marvin's lifelong pet project was to bare the secrecies and unfairness surrounding book jobbers' pricing schedules. He wrote about this often.

Life after death in Judaism is an amorphous reality that some believe in. But almost all Jews believe that life after death is embedded in the idea of remembering and memorializing the life of the deceased. In this sense at least, Marvin is still alive to many of us. Although we grow older and forget much about the recent past, many of us will never forget Marvin's deep, lasting impact on our lives. Marvin made a difference and left his mark. May it continue.

Notes

1. Rosten, Leo Calvin, *The Education of H*Y*M*A*N K*A*P*L*A*N* (New York: Harcourt Brace, 1937).
2. Rosten, *The Education of H*Y*M*A*N K*A*P*L*A*N*, 174, 176.

Chapter 12

Marvin Scilken: A Remembrance of Him as an ALA Colleague

Peggy Sullivan

It has been three years since Marvin Scilken died, and I have thought of him often during these past months. I know that I am only one of many who have. At conferences and midwinter meetings of the American Library Association (ALA), people frequently say, "Imagine what Marvin would say!" or "Marvin should be here to hear that!" With all its bigness and complexity, ALA has many of the characteristics of a small town, and people are remembered and cherished, especially if they have brought the inimitable qualities that Marvin Scilken brought to ALA.

I now realize that there were many parts of Marvin's life I did not know. I got to know him as a person only after he became a member of ALA Council. I have been charmed to learn that he had engaged in another career for a decade or so before enrolling in library school.

It comes as no surprise that he saw the advertisement recruiting librarians in the *New York Times*. He was an enthusiastic reader of the *Times* and quoted it and wrote to it frequently throughout his life. If he was the only person recruited from that small ad, it was surely worth it. He brought to librarianship enthusiasm and commitment, a desire to serve others, and an ability to inspire others to share his vision. I have to believe that there was all too little opportunity to exercise any of those characteristics in his prior work as a manager of personal credit.

Often, when people embark on second careers, they view their studies as tickets to new jobs. I cannot imagine that Marvin did so. His graduation from the history-rich library school at Pratt Institute and his initiation into Beta Phi Mu, the international library honorary society, are evidence that he did not. I can see Marvin as a challenging, inquisitive student, wanting to get from the experience every bit of value that he could. I am sure that faculty and fellow students remember him a colleague with something special to offer.

Again, it is no surprise that Marvin chose public librarianship. He brought to it a much-needed passion that is all too rare. As someone who has worked in a variety of libraries, library association staff work, and library education during my own career, I can appreciate Marvin's commitment to public librarianship. A couple of years ago, a former student met me on the street, and said, "I know you can't answer this here, but I am going to call you and ask you what your favorite kind of library is—since you've been in so many." I immediately said, "No need to call me back! I worked in four different public libraries for a total of fourteen years, and public library work is by far my favorite kind. That's where the action is!" To be honest, I have had more satisfying jobs in other settings from time to time, but public libraries have a very special place in my heart. I know that had to be true for Marvin as well, and he lived up to his commitment by spending his career in public libraries.

The moves that Marvin made early in his career among public libraries near New York City led inevitably to his position as library director of the Orange Public Library in New Jersey. It offered him the diversity of clientele, the challenges of change, and the size to make a real difference to the community—and he did just that.

I first heard of Marvin Scilken through the *U*N*A*B*A*S*H*E*D Librarian*, which he started to publish in 1971. I have to admit that I never became a regular reader or subscriber until I was Assistant Commissioner of The Chicago Public Library from 1977–1981. There I worked with some of the best and brightest younger colleagues I ever knew who frequently provided me with references or clippings from the *U*N*A*B*A*S*H*E*D Librarian*. It provided many librarians with a kind of community and a sense of belonging. It was and still is a forum for many practitioners to share their working knowledge solving grass-roots problems. Marvin encouraged young librarians to contribute to his quarterly. For many, it was their first opportunity to publish, and it got them started sharing ideas and viewpoints with the encouragement and appreciation of a committed editor. In some respects, the *U*N*A*B*A*S*H*E*D Librarian* was counter-cultural, providing ideas that could be implemented regardless of a library's more formal protocols.

When I asked a distinguished colleague recently about some of his memories of Marvin, he, of course, focused on the quarterly that he had read from his very early days in librarianship. Marvin was always encouraging him to write for the *U*N*A*B*A*S*H*E*D Librarian*. He never did, but it made him feel good to be sought out like that, and he in turn had encouraged others to write. What a great legacy for one to leave!

I do not for a moment believe that Marvin carefully planned his career. He had good judgment and ambition. He possessed enough confidence and knowledge of himself to accomplish what he wanted to do. He attended his first

ALA Annual Conference in Montreal in 1960. That was a good beginning. The Canadian setting brought greater visibility to the international role of the association. Our Canadian colleagues, many of whom were longtime ALA members, were delightful hosts. ALA had not met in Canada since 1934, so it was an especially celebratory conference. I would like to think that I ran into Marvin there or saw him moving through the exhibits, but I didn't. From that point on, he set out to attend ALA conferences on a regular basis and quickly attracted a host of new friends and acquaintances. His press pass allowed him considerable opportunity to reach behind the scenes of conferences, programs, and meetings of membership units and committees.

A major event in Marvin's professional life was speaking on behalf of libraries before the Senate Subcommittee on Antitrust and Monopoly's hearing on price fixing by publishers. He led the way with very little organized support and great skepticism from others that anything positive might come of it. He studied the issue carefully and attempted to get support from library groups, but essentially he went it alone. His efforts led to libraries recovering millions of dollars.

It is my guess that it was this successful effort that led Marvin to consider becoming a member of ALA's Council. Some dismiss the policymaking body of about 150 members as a poorly organized group of overly talkative people. I happen to love Council myself and served a total of seven years. But I have spent far more time observing Council than participating in it. The amount of reading material that one typically receives before Council meetings can flummox many less-hardy members. Still, issues that appear before Council relate to many aspects of librarianship, and the diversity of Council members ensures a wide range of opinions.

Marvin saw Council's potential to help him achieve his goals and express his opinions. He was elected to five four-year terms as a Councilor-at-large beginning in 1981.

Marvin enjoyed the give and take of Council discussions. He often sat by the aisle to have easier access to the microphones. He never seemed embarrassed to say when he did not understand something, but it was also often a ploy to call attention to some detail that needed clarification. Marvin was in his element in Council.

Marvin chose to focus on the issues that meant the most to him. He was passionate about publishers' unfair treatment of libraries. When the name of Dan Lacy, former chief executive of the American Book Publishers Council, was proposed for honorary ALA membership, Marvin was forceful in his opposition. He undoubtedly provided leadership to others who spoke and voted against this recognition. They succeeded in denying Lacy the honor, an embarrassment for Lacy and for those who had proposed it. Council usually approves such proposals by a unanimous vote, and Marvin was surely the point man on this dramatic rejection.

On one occasion, a Councilor mentioned that his constituency had urged him to speak and vote in a certain way. Marvin got up to say that since he was a Councilor-at-Large he received no instructions from his constituency. He garnered some good-natured ribbing. Other Councilors said that people wrote or called them often to urge them to vote in a certain way. Marvin looked genuinely puzzled and repeated that he had never been so approached. Most likely those who knew Marvin and voted for him sensed that his judgment, his ability to think on his feet, and his dedicated preparation for Council meetings meant they did not have to tell him how they felt or what they expected him to do. He inspired and retained their trust.

Partly because of his informal dress, Marvin projected the image of a man who came prepared to work. In speaking with people about their memories of Marvin, they almost always mention how well prepared he was to tackle the many issues with which Council dealt. There was one issue that he returned to repeatedly: the matter of sites for ALA Annual Conferences and Midwinter Meetings. More than once, Marvin went to the microphone to bemoan the fact that summer conferences were scheduled in the hottest cities and Midwinters were all too often in the coldest cities. The ALA Executive Board—and not Council—decides on conference sites. One could rely on Marvin to express his feelings strongly when these decisions were announced to Council. His persistence led to the appointment of a committee to review the matter. Staff and officers always reminded Council that decisions about sites were made after considering issues such as costs for members' housing and availability of the acres of space required for programs, committee meetings, social functions, and exhibits. But in this area, as in many others, Marvin clung to his convictions and became associated with a strong, well-expressed point of view.

Even Marvin's style in Council was informal. In effect he often said, "I just don't get it! How can people think this way?" His own good nature meant that people listened to him and extended him the courtesy he showed others. Even when they disagreed with him, they appreciated what he had to say and how he said it.

It was natural for Marvin to consider running for ALA President. He recognized the value of the presidency as a platform for his views. He saw it as an opportunity to move ALA toward acting on the concerns he believed in most. In the fall of 1990, the ALA Nominating Committee announced the names of two candidates, Marilyn Miller of the University of North Carolina at Greensboro and Charles Bunge of the University of Wisconsin at Madison. Both were library educators with long experience in ALA. When the opportunity came for petition candidates to be added to the slate, there were two more: Herbert White, a library educator from Indiana University, and Marvin Scilken from the Orange Public Library.

The petition candidates, or those supporting them, ask ALA members to sign a petition to have their names added to the ballot. Those who have sought the presidency in recent years have usually petitioned before the Midwinter Meeting since at Midwinter candidates often speak to various boards and participate in a candidates' forum, using the meeting to advance their campaign.

Predictably, Marvin wanted change in ALA. He was especially concerned about its cozy collaboration with publishers and other vendors. When he arrived at a Midwinter Council meeting wearing a suit, he must have been ready for surprised looks and joshing remarks, but that change in his style showed how serious he was about his candidacy.

ALA elections are often difficult to predict. Voters consider where candidates live, the area of librarianship they represent, their presentations at Midwinter, their experiences within the association, their genders and lifestyles, their ages and experiences, and their writings.

Four-way elections are even more difficult to predict. In the 1991 election, in a field of three men and one woman, none of whom had served on the ALA Executive Board (another characteristic often weighed in), Marilyn Miller won by a narrow margin over Herbert White, 3,939 votes to 3,896. The other person nominated by the ALA Nominating Committee, Charles Bunge, was third with 2,982 votes, and Marvin trailed with 2,190 votes.

When Marvin next ran for reelection to Council, he received an amazingly high number of votes (4,788). One interpretation of this is that many people, probably even many who had not supported him for the ALA Presidency, wanted to show their appreciation of his participation in Council, in spite of his loss in the presidential election.

Marvin was a member of Council during the two years that I served as ALA Executive Director from 1992 to 1994. I had the unusual opportunity to view him from the platform during Council meetings and to be the target of some of his discomfort and disappointment with the way ALA worked—or, as Marvin would probably say, the way it didn't work!

When a hurricane swept through Florida, Marvin called me at ALA Headquarters to say that he thought I should hire a truck, fill it with books, and drive through the stricken areas providing reading for those made homeless or otherwise inconvenienced by the emergency. He thought that somebody should do it and that it should probably be the ALA Executive Director. It would be good public relations for the association, he said, and it would be a good way for me really to get out there and see what was going on.

I told Marvin that I would not be following up on his suggestion, but the conversation reminded me to check with other staff to see what kinds of help and information the association was providing to libraries and the public in the devastated areas. I discovered that most of our efforts were directed at getting information from libraries about their status and assisting them in any way we could. To my surprise, I also learned that several staff members had also received calls from Marvin urging them to write articles, provide him with information and listen to his ideas. They commented that he was a frequent caller on many topics. He did not wait for Council meetings to express his opinions.

In the early 1990s Council was moving toward using email for informal communications between sessions. Marilyn Miller, while presiding at Council, invited members to provide their email addresses so that a Council listserv could be created. Within the next few years, the listserv became the medium of choice for the many discussions and notes that Council needed. Marvin was one of the last holdouts. He was moving toward retirement, and he had communicated so consistently and successfully over the years that he probably just didn't get excited about learning to use email.

Marvin was still serving on Council when I left the Executive Directorship, and we returned to more pleasant, more casual conversations, mostly during ALA meetings and conferences. Marvin had advice for me about retirement. He told me that when he worked at Orange, he had not realized how much of the time he was on his feet moving around the library. He cautioned me to exercise regularly to stay healthy. I remember that I told him that I walked regularly and that on alternate days I exercised, mostly to strengthen my knees. The next time I saw him, months later, he was moving through a convention center with his wife, Polly. When we stopped to talk, I told him that I was still exercising, just as he had told me to do. Polly scoffed, "Why, Marvin doesn't exercise at all!" Marvin may have been a little red-faced, but after all his advice was good, and I was following it. So what was there to be concerned about?

Marvin's death occurred during the night of one of his active days at an ALA Midwinter Meeting. I guessed afterwards that Polly Scilken attended ALA meetings with him in his later years so that she could watch out for his health. Marvin was proud of her career in nursing and nursing education. He once referred me to her when I was conducting a search for a chair of the School of Nursing at Northern Illinois University while I was dean of their College of Professional Studies. He assured me that Polly was a respected leader in nursing and undoubtedly could suggest good candidates. My telephone conversation with her then was our first introduction to each other. I enjoyed getting to know her in the later years when she became a devoted Council-watcher, which, of course, also meant being a Marvin-watcher.

When one sees only a single aspect of another's work, the full picture of their professional work and personal life is obscured. Marvin was an administrator with many commitments and achievements. He participated in the New Jersey Library Association as well as in ALA. He founded and made a success of the U*N*A*B*A*S*H*E*D Librarian. He was devoted to his family. He prided himself, appropriately enough, on being a gadfly and a conscience for others. In ALA, as in so many of his other activities, Marvin Scilken was a generous giver.

Chapter 13

A Memory of Marvin Scilken: How We Met in Minnesota Thirty-Plus Years Ago

Maurice J. ("Mitch") Freedman

The following is a slightly edited version of the comments Maurice J. Freedman contributed at the American Library Association Council memorial service for Marvin Scilken held during the 1999 Midwinter meeting in Philadelphia on February 3, a few hours after Marvin passed away.

It was about twenty-five below zero. I was working at the Hennepin County Library. I don't remember whether it was 1969 or 1970, but there was a conference in St. Paul at Macalester College. Dan Gore, the librarian from Macalester, and Marvin were the two speakers for the program. They were speaking about ways to make library service better. Now this is not a put-down of Dan Gore. It is just indicative that, of the two of them, Marvin stayed with this mission his entire life.

This was his avocation, this was his vocation. Aside from his love for his family and his time with his family, he, more than anybody I know, lived being a librarian. And his retirement made no difference whatsoever.

When I worked at the New York Public Library (NYPL), I was head of technical services for the Branch Libraries. I don't know if any of you have had the pleasure of being antagonized by Marvin. I think antagonizing people was something he delighted in, whether he was conscious of this or not. He would telephone me repeatedly and keep working at me about the poor service he received at one of the NYPL branches until he reached my pressure point. I told him repeatedly that as head of tech services I had virtually no role in branch services.

Kay Cassell in her earlier remarks today only touched the surface of Marvin's indictment of the New York Public Library Branch Libraries. He would report every heinous crime—at least in his opinion—against the library's users at the branches that he visited. And he visited a lot of them. As I said, at a certain point I really got tired of the phone calls. I said, "Do you want to tell me how technical services is a mess, Marvin? I'll be glad to hear it. But if I had any control over the branches I'd work at improvements with my heart and soul, Marvin, just to shut you up if nothing else."

It really was offensive to him when a librarian would sit at a desk reading a book. Then when a patron came up and asked for some help, the librarian would look up briefly, say, "Look it up in the catalog," and go back to reading. That was one of Marvin's complaints that stuck in my mind. Marvin was right to be offended.

And I don't think there was anybody, to repeat myself, more dedicated, more loving of libraries.

He was an inveterate letter writer. Marvin was really a full service non-discriminating critic because whatever he read, saw, or heard about was the subject of his review. And if he decided it was wrong, he fired off a letter. Dan O'Connor's article on Marvin in the *Second Supplement to the Dictionary of American Library Biography* gives the reader an idea of the breadth of publications in which his letters appeared—everything from the *New York Times* to an airline magazine.

One of the words he loved and frequently used—which I think I never, ever used in my whole life—was the word "nifty." When Marvin called something nifty, he was assigning the highest possible compliment. That was really nifty.

And he was always there with his camera. God knows, Polly, how many cameras will be his legacy in your house. It seemed that every year or two he'd show up with a new camera. I treasure the photos he sent me. And I am grateful that he had someone take a Polaroid of himself and me. I was able to use that for the cover of issue number 114 of the *U*N*A*B*A*S*H*E*D Librarian, the "How I Run My Library Good" Letter,* the first one I published.

It was just last year Polly and Marvin came up from Manhattan to the Book and Author Luncheon the Westchester Library System runs every year. They had already signed up and sent a check for this year's luncheon. We had just moved into our new quarters. Marvin came with his camera and took pictures with great happiness. I have a picture of me in front of the bare walls and the cartons that still hadn't been unpacked. He sent me these pictures as he sent others over the years.

The man was filled with love for the profession. His love also extended most especially to his friends. I have no idea—and I think how little idea anyone else had—of how many people Marvin touched. I know the circle of friends and the particular area of overlap that I'm in. His friends extend from the then dean of Pratt, to a book seller, to the head of one of the libraries in the City University of New York, and God only knows how many people from New Jersey, the rest of the country, and the world. His retirement dinner must have had at least a couple of hundred attendees. It's endless the people he touched—a truth confirmed by the number and range of people who just told their own stories of their special relationships with Marvin this morning.

The thing that struck me about Marvin was he never grew old as a librarian. He never aged as a librarian. He was fresh in his advocacy for public service. It fact, it wasn't even public service that he advocated. It was simpler than that. He was an advocate for the user. For Marvin, the user is holy. According to Marvin, we librarians have no basis for existence—nor does the library as an institution have any basis for existence, none of it means a thing—unless we're totally and wholly dedicated to serving the user. He took that belief to technical services, to reference work, everywhere in the library. And that was what his "how I run my library good letter" was all about.

His passion for serving the user is the legacy Marvin has given us. I will do my very best to live up to it. Rest in peace, Marvin. I love you.

Notes

1. Donald G. Davis, Jr., ed. *Second Supplement to the Dictionary of American Library Biography* (Englewood, Colo.: Libraries Unlimited, in press), s.v. "Scilken, Marvin H. (1926–1999)."

Chapter 14

Marvin Scilken in the Bronx

Marjorie Scilken-Friedman

Let me give you a picture of family life with Marvin Scilken, my brother. Our parents came from Russia twenty years before the period I am writing about, the 1930s to the 1940s. Our father settled in the lower East Side and worked up from a vendor's stall to a small grocery store, to a suit-and-tie-job as a star salesman for General Electric, and then to marriage and, having made it, to a significant move to the Bronx.

We, like many Jewish families of the time, had retreated to discover that still rural Bronx near a reservoir bordered by rock outcroppings and parks. Ours was a new, not always welcome, ethnic influx. At the time, Irish Catholics had already established their homes and political turf in the Bronx.

I can remember that some streets were like borders. We lived in a large apartment house at 2865 University Avenue that had a back exit. There was a church and Catholic school on that block, and we just didn't go in or out that exit unless we felt the need to engage in battle in the playground on that corner.

As children in this emerging middle-class setting, little of the experience of the larger world trickled into our home. We could listen to the radio, but there was no book-lined study. Our parents were both unusually inventive and creative, but neither our mother nor our father were educated beyond grade school.

The schools were preparing us for life in the United States, but there was no one to turn to to help reconcile the differences between home and school. Each setting expected strict behavior, and the codes of one often contradicted the morals of the other. Although this life situation might still remain true for children of immigrant parents, no computer, Internet or television bridged home this new culture for us.

The blank screen of the 1930s provided the intense need for the *library*. We didn't have to walk ten miles along a dirt road to get to a one-room schoolhouse, but we did walk four miles or so down paved streets to get to our library. In my mind, I can still walk through those streets and around the corners to the Bainbridge Avenue Branch Library, now called the Fordham Library Center Branch of the New York Public Library.

Did Marvin and I go together? If I say now that we did, there would be no one to contradict me. From 2865 University Avenue we walked toward Jerome Avenue and the elevated Kingsbridge Road train station, slowly around a massive red brick medieval building, the Kingsbridge Armory. This was a huge, mysterious structure with story-book turrets. We ambled across and under the dark elevated tracks at the Kingsbridge Road Station and several blocks up to the Grand Concourse lined with bench-sitting elders. Poe's Cottage was back there in the greenery. Then we headed toward Fordham Road where stood a series of stone steps down to the Bainbridge Avenue Branch Library. The library had been renovated in 1931, and there was a separate children's area on the lower floor. I can vouchsafe that we read through all those books well before we reached the age—whatever it was—that entitled us to an adult card and that trek upstairs to the main section. I can remember finishing all the Zane Grey's there were. Marvin must have had a similar experience.

When Marvin spoke about our childhood, he would tell friends that we were brought up as "only children." He had been fragile, dark-haired with a speech impediment, and my mother was very protective and nurturing of him. I can remember Marvin getting special egg creams so he could put on weight. I can also recall Mother's visits to school on his behalf. Teachers didn't understand that his reluctance to speak out then did not mean he didn't know the material.

Finally, I can recall one battle Marvin and I had. It was over a heavy old typewriter. I think I was on it too long and Marvin wanted it. Or perhaps it was something else. But I still have that vision of fragile little Marvin picking up that bulky square Underwood, preparing to toss it out the window.

Chapter 15

Desperately Seeking Marvin[1]

Karen G. Schneider

A funny thing happened on my way to interview Marvin Scilken, an articulate, urbane, retired librarian and editor of the ever-useful U*N*A*B*A*S*H*E*D Librarian, (subtitled, "The 'How I Run My Library Good' Letter," and one of the last librarians not connected to the Internet (at least according to the two dozen e-mail messages I received identifying him as an online Johnny-Come-Lately). With the technical assistance of Dean Seoud Matta and Charles Rubenstein of Pratt Institute's School of Information and Library Science, Marvin was finally about to go online; so I needed to get to him quickly, while his unwired status still applied.

I was sure that I could persuade Marvin that he really needed the Internet. However, after two days of phone and fax interviews (the first time I haven't used e-mail to interview someone for this column), I came to a rather humbling conclusion: it's not that Marvin needs the Internet—he probably doesn't—but that the Internet needs Marvin.

We need Marvin online in part because his experience is a reminder that the Internet is just one more information/communication medium, and one that is only as good as its content and organization. Marvin lives in New York, a town sparkling with cultural treasures, where it's easy to lead an intellectually rich life without the Internet. Marvin, busy with a vigorous lifelong reading habit, news discussion groups, visits to museums, and concerts, not to mention his journalistic duties (which include sending frequent letters-to-the-editor of the New York Times), can't quite figure out where the Internet fits into this busy life, and who can blame him?

Phoning for Flowers

During his initial sojourn online, Marvin tried to find the date of the Cherry Blossom Festival at the Brooklyn Botanic Garden and information about national wildflower-related activities. Though this information is on the Web, it wasn't easily or quickly accessible to Marvin, who ended up using the phone. It doesn't help that Marvin can't type and that's not uncommon among older people, not to mention those who can't see or don't have use of their hands. We make a lot of assumptions when we offer information online.

The other reason we need Marvin online and all the other older and retired librarians has to do with librarianship in general, and the particular communication activities that the Internet enables. Our two days of interviews were a crash course for me on a range of topics from adult-user behavior to intellectual freedom. Nothing teaches like the wisdom of someone who has been in the trenches since Melvil Dewey was a circ clerk.

Promotional Positions

We had a long debate about the best approach to promoting America's libraries (Marvin favors paying for ad space in major papers, as Albert Shanker's blurbs for the United Federation of Teachers did for twenty-five years, while I lean toward a Madison Avenue "Got Milk?" approach). Marvin was startled to discover that librarians had carried on exactly this discussion on Web4Lib and I bet most librarians on Web4Lib would be startled to discover that Marvin, an at-large ALA Council member, had submitted the idea of an ad campaign at this year's ALA presidential candidates forum, as he has several times in the past.

Marvin was also surprised to discover that many publications currently have free online counterparts. The fact that this is news to Marvin is something else to heed; how well have we communicated to our senior and retired librarians what the Internet really offers, and do we help them get online? Maybe we need to ditch the traditional gold watches in favor of Pentiums with modems and a few hours of training.

Marvin's skepticism is instructive. Noting that most adult out-of-school public library users "read for pleasure," Marvin shared his test for the validity of any library service, which he calls Scilken's Law: "If the service in question was the only service offered, could the library get local tax dollars to do it?" Before you jump up to defend the Internet, pay attention: Marvin was referring to reference services and I think he has a point. A public library that offered only reference services, however important they are, wouldn't survive long. He thinks video lending "might make it" in some communities, as would, of course, books. As for the Internet, unless the book is replaced by a networked digital equivalent, which won't happen soon, even I a militant cyber-booster can't see a community funding an Internet-only public library.

Marvin's point is not that we shouldn't use the Internet or offer it to our patrons; he's talking about understanding what the public wants and tailoring our services and our messages accordingly so the people get the services they want and we get the funding we need. That's a good message in responsible pragmatism to share with the young pups fresh out of library school.

A final note: several days after I interviewed Marvin, the *New York Times* published a letter on Internet filters that Marvin had encouraged me to write. Because of the interest generated by this letter, I started a Web-based project (at http://www.bluehighways.com/tifap.htm), which caught my book editor's eye; so now I'm writing a book (*A Practical Guide to Internet Filters*, due out late summer from Neal-Schuman).

Meanwhile, a few days after that, I received an e-mail from Marvin asking for better instructions for subscribing to library-related discussion lists, and pretty soon I saw his e-mail address sail into the PUBLIB database. We both gained from sharing our skills and experiences. As for the Brooklyn Botanical Garden It's still just another pretty Web site; if they're smart, they'll hire Marvin as a usability consultant.

This Month's Web Sites

National Wildflower Research Center, http://www.wildflower.org/ (1 Sept. 2001).
Brooklyn Botanical Garden, http://www.bbg.org/ (1 Sept. 2001).
Web4Lib, http://sunsite.berkeley.edu/Web4Lib/ (1 Sept. 2001).

Notes

1. Karen G. Schneider. "Desperately Seeking Marvin." *American Libraries* 28, no. 6 (June/July 1997): 116.

Chapter 16

The Elements of Marvin[1]

Karen G. Schneider

Two years ago I had the privilege of interviewing Marvin Scilken for a column.[2] Among his many claims to fame, Marvin, during and after his long career as a public library director, was the editor of the *U*N*A*B*A*S*H*E*D Librarian (U*L)*, a small, homespun newsletter of practical advice subtitled *The 'How I Run My Library Good' Letter.*

Polly Scilken, Marvin's widow and faithful editorial assistant for all these years, is publishing the next two issues on her own; the future of *U*L* is then uncertain, but Polly knows she wants it to continue, and so do many of us in Libraryland. A couple of people suggested to me that we don't need *U*L* any more because we have Internet discussion groups such as PUBLIB and Stumpers. But I again measured the entire Internet against one Marvin Scilken, and I again came up short by the barrelful.

The Beauty of Tangibility

The *U*N*A*B*A*S*H*E*D Librarian* had the beauty of tangibility. You could touch it, feel it, shove it in a backpack, prop it on a treadmill, circle good ideas and stuff it in a colleague's mailbox in a way you simply cannot do with our electronic forums such as PUBLIB.

The (irregular, always late) arrival of *U*L* was a silent rebuke to all things digital (and hence intangible). Marvin wrote it—literally, in longhand, while Polly typed out the columns (I don't mean keyboarded, I mean typed). It was "cut and paste" in the old-fashioned sense. If you looked closely enough, you could see the evidence of its analog origins: a slight skewing here and there, the faint shadow of paper pasted on paper, or a font change. Even the asterisks between the letters—borrowed from *The Education of H*Y*M*A*N K*A*P*L*A*N*, Leo Rosten's achingly funny book about a postwar immigrant's struggle to learn English—were humorous in part because they were a product of a real typewriter.[3] Like watching your breath spiral from your mouth on a cold winter's day, *U*L* was evidence itself of the beautifully concrete world that Marvin knew was our first, our only real inhabitance.

The Comfort of Closure

Internet discussion groups are just that—ongoing discussions. Like a Robert Altman movie, we chatter and chatter. Go away for a few weeks and sign on again, and we are all still chattering, unfettered by page length, editorial deadlines, or, for that matter, editors. This has its advantages. But we are also creatures of habit who seek patterns and closure in our lives, and the arrival of a new issue of a magazine, with its beginning, middle and end, its specificity, its limits, is a small but noticeable ceremony in our lives—one we should consider carefully before abandoning it to an endlessly gurgling stream of digitized information.

Our library district now has access to the EBSCOhost database, a commercial internet database with hundreds of full-text magazine articles. While we all find it useful and fun, EBSCOhost isn't really designed for browsing by issue. One patron commented, "I guess I'm being old-fashioned—I want to read a magazine." I said I knew exactly what he meant, and we talked about the joy of "the latest issue": the ceremonial inspection of the cover, the quick glance at the table of contents, the rapid assessment of one's calendar to determine how soon you can hunker down and without interruption enjoy your treat. Marvin, the cagey old press man, knew that librarians wanted to read a real, finite magazine—especially a magazine about them.

Since I am known to respond, instantly and at luxurious length, to any stray idea I happen to encounter on the Internet, you may well raise your eyebrows when I say that the advantage of *U*L* over a discussion group was that it was highly selective. Discussion groups are wonderful because they are all over the map: posting guidelines usually ask only that you don't break laws or cause fights. But *U*L* was the first distillation of Marvin's review of many, many newsletters, talks he had with people, and "reporting assignments" he sent people on.

As Sue Kamm, librarian at Los Angeles Public and erstwhile *U*L* stringer, put it, the publication was a careful selection of "nuggets of wisdom"—bibliographies, bookmarks, programming ideas—that if nothing else would be difficult to ferret out from the flotsam of most discussion lists. Terrific graphics often accompanied the discussion. Michael Golrick of the Southern Connecticut Library Council said, "I recently had occasion to look through the last eight or so issues. In every one, there was some very clear graphic 'cut and paste' of a library's great idea." You can't get that from discussion lists.

Marvin skimmed the cream of the very best of current library practice and shared it in his coarse little cut-and-paste magazine, and we are all the worse for its loss. We don't have to close the door on "that type" of library newsletter, though. Rory Litwin is the editor of a little library e-mail newsletter called *Library Juice* (www.libr.org/Juice)—not a library management newsletter, but a compilation of current issues and news. Through Rory's lens, you see an alternative view of librarianship—maybe not one you agree with, but an interesting view all the same. Despite its electronic format, it has a feeling very similar to *U*L*—homey and very human. (Where else can you learn about bellydancing librarians?) We need more Marvins and Rorys, and we need to continue our tradition of the little newsletters that could. They feed our need for all that is tangible, finite, and selective, and bring us back to earth.

Notes

1. Karen G. Schneider. "The Elements of Marvin." *American Libraries* 30, no. 4 (April 1999): 88.
2. Karen G. Schneider, "Desperately Seeking Marvin," *American Libraries* 28, no. 6 (June/July 1997): 116.
3. Rosten, Leo Calvin, *The Education of H*Y*M*A*N K*A*P*L*A*N* (New York: Harcourt, Brace and Company, 1937).

Chapter 17

Marvin Scilken:
A Biographical Sketch and a Personal
Reflection

Matthew Mantel

Marvin Scilkem was best known as the editor and publisher of the
U*N*A*B*A*S*H*E*D Librarian (*U*L*), "a small, homespun newsletter of
practical advice subtitled, "The 'How I Run My Library Good' Letter."[1] This
quarterly newsletter, typed by Marvin's wife, Polly Scilken, is a compendium of
practical library wisdom sent in by working librarians. Marvin's editorial
philosophy was to include nothing too "theoretical, speculative, or too
scholarly.[2] Marvin and *U*L* collected all those simple and not so simple items
and thoughts that library school did not teach you and disseminated them around
the world. *U*L* focuses "on the need for better public relations [and] show[s] how
librarians can make their services and skills more visible to the public."[3] Marvin
believed that "the library must be wholly dedicated to the user."[4] As he said, "we
are in the book business. What we should do is give people all the books they
want as quickly as we can with as hassle-free service as possible."[5]

Marvin was nearly as famous for his editorial letters, many of which
appeared in the *New York Times*. Marvin never let pass an opportunity to
publicize libraries and their services, be it a letter advising potential car buyers to
visit the library to arm themselves with the proper information or a letter to
Jeopardy host Alex Trebek suggesting that blow-ups of the contestants' hometown library cards be displayed on their podiums to publicize their local libraries.

Although Trebek mentioned the letter on the air, the idea has yet to be implemented.[6]

One of Marvin's lesser-known accomplishments is his testimony before the Senate Subcommittee on Antitrust and Monopoly in 1962. As a result of Marvin's testimony on publisher price fixing, libraries pursued over one thousand lawsuits against publishers and recovered over $10 million. Marvin also helped pass ALA resolutions requesting publishers give libraries discounts equivalent to those given to booksellers for comparable orders. As Marvin eloquently stated, "instead of libraries subsidizing publishers, perhaps publishers should subsidize libraries for the services they perform in maintaining and enlarging America's book-reading public." Marvin also convinced Bell Atlantic to give libraries free copies of out-of-state telephone directories.[7]

Marvin was the quintessential librarian-as-gadfly. He was truly an unabashed librarian, doing what he could, and helping others do what they could, to improve libraries for the people who use them. As Marvin put it in his no-nonsense manner, "Give the people what they want. It's their library." [8]

How do I know all this? Marvin was the subject of my first research assignment in library school. After five years on the law practice merry-go-round I thought it was time to jump off, and I landed in the library world. Our first project was to research and write about a famous or influential person in the library profession. Not knowing many names beyond Melvil Dewey and Andrew Carnegie, I chose the most interesting name—or rather the second most interesting one. The Balkan name of a professor at Rutgers looked better on the page but had the misfortune of being virtually unpronounceable. So Marvin Scilken it was.

Upon picking the name (out of the proverbial hat) I learned that he published something called the U*N*A*B*A*S*H*E*D Librarian. Right. I took this information home and consulted a relative in the library business who verified that indeed such a publication did exist and that yes it was quite well known. Now secure that I was not the subject of a cruel library school prank, I headed off to the building that gave my new profession its name and began to burrow into the life of Marvin Scilken.

I got the basics from a variety of interviews conducted with Marvin over the years and from reading issues of U*L. Then I read of his testimony before Congress as a witness against the pricing practices of large publishing houses. The testimony precipitated lawsuits and judgments in favor of libraries. I read the letters he sent to the New York Times giving readers advice on how to best utilize their libraries. It was clear that to Marvin the library belonged to the reader and not to the librarian. His letters always sought to market the public library. His Jeopardy idea, for example, was one of Marvin's most creative.

I also found that Marvin and I had a lot in common. We were both Yankees who had gone out West to get our education—he to Colorado and I to Texas. I discovered that his own library was in New Jersey where I had grown up. The day before I presented my paper on Marvin I had flown back to Texas from visiting family in New Jersey. If it hadn't been snowing during my stay in New Jersey I might even have made a pilgrimage to Marvin's library for extra credit. Most of all I found that we were both advocates. As an attorney I had been an advocate for my injured clients. Marvin had spent his life as an advocate for libraries. Marvin argued hard to get the public to recognize the value of their own library and to use it for all it was worth. But Marvin's advocacy did not end there.

By publishing U*L Marvin also pointed his deadly accurate bullshit detector at the members of his own profession. He simply wanted librarians to "run their libraries good." He sought to produce a compendium of practical library wisdom sent in by working librarians. Marvin wanted librarians to run their libraries to benefit their patrons, to get books into their hands. Anything that furthered that job was good; anything that subtracted from that job was bad.

I had always considered myself a very practical lawyer. My job was to help my clients without wasting their time or their money, and that is what I did. Marvin Scilken practiced librarianship as I practiced law. He was dedicated to his client (or patron, or user, or reader; take your pick). He was a positive influence on his colleagues and an advocate for his profession. He served his clients well.

In law school our professors exhorted us to follow the great lawyers and justices of the past—John Marshall, Earl Warren, and Thurgood Marshall. These men reshaped their vocation and our culture. I never met the man, but in my new profession, Marvin Scilken was a role model on par with them. New librarians could do a lot worse than reading what Marvin had to say: "Give the people what they want. It's their library."[9]

Notes

1. The U*N*A*B*A*S*H*E*D L*I*B*R*A*R*I*A*N, no 110 (1999): 2.

2. Karen G. Schneider, "The Elements of Marvin," American Libraries 30, no. 4 (April 1999): 88.

3. Joseph Deitch, "Portrait: Marvin Scilken," Wilson Library Bulletin 59, No. 3 (November 1994): 206.

4. Ellen Zyroff and Jack Forman, "Will Marvin's Legacy be Placed in Jeopardy?" American Libraries 30, no. 5 (May 1999): 40.

5. Deitch, "Portrait: Marvin Scilken," 207.

6. Zyroff and Forman, "Will Marvin's Legacy be Placed in Jeopardy?" 88.

7. "Popular Scilken Dies Suddenly in Philly," Library Journal 124, no. 4 (1 March 1999): 13

8. Deitch, "Portrait: Marvin Scilken," 207.

9. Deitch, "Portrait: Marvin Scilken," 207.

Bibliography

Selected Publications by and about Marvin H. Scilken

Holly M. King

Marvin Scilken was a passionate and tireless advocate for libraries, as the materials written by and about him make clear. The following bibliography is divided into four sections: items Scilken wrote for his quarterly newsletter, the *U*N*A*B*A*S*H*E*D Librarian* (*U*L*); articles written for other publications; some of Scilken's many letters to journals, magazines, and newspapers; and articles written by others about Scilken. Items are arranged by publication date; earliest publications are listed first.

This bibliography's longest section is its first one. Scilken edited and published *U*L* for almost thirty years—from 1971 until his death in February 1999. Though plain in appearance, *U*L* was filled with useful material related to libraries and librarianship, with many contributions from other librarians. Content included practical suggestions and advice, bibliographies and booklists, humor, satire, letters, reprinted articles, excerpts, sample forms and flyers, and information on topics such as cataloging, publishing, public relations, library programs, policies, and procedures—as Scilken said, anything of interest or use to libraries. Each issue featured editorial notes ("Editor's Mumblings") and comments. In addition to serving as editor, Scilken contributed more than 170 pieces to *U*L*. His writings, as well as the other materials appearing in this bibliography, give ample evidence of Marvin Scilken's undying belief in "working to get libraries the credit they deserve." (This was Scilken's slogan when he ran for president of the American Library Association in 1991.)

Articles from the *U*N*A*B*A*S*H*E*D Librarian*

Scilken, Marvin H. "Cards, Extra, What to Do With." *U*L*, no. 1 (November 1971): 6.
———. "Catchwords, Subtitles, and Synthetic Subtitles." *U*L*, no. 1 (November 1971): 32.
———. "Changing Subject Headings." *U*L*, no. 1 (November 1971): 26.
———. "The Civil Service Test Book Problem (or Turning Turner Out)." *U*L*, no. 1 (November 1971): 14–15.
———. "Ending Subject/Title Confusion." *U*L*, no. 1 (November 1971): 10.
———. "Filing Subject Cards by Date." *U*L*, no. 1 (November 1971): 3.
———. "Getting It All Together (on the Shelf)." *U*L*, no. 1 (November 1971): 9.
———. "High Loss List." *U*L*, no. 1 (November 1971): 4–6.
———. "An Only-One-Writing Charging Form for Pamphlets." *U*L*, no. 1 (November 1971): 20–21.
———. "Prisons—U.S. to Prue (Some Thought on Replacing the Cards in a Missing Catalog Tray)." *U*L*, no. 1 (November 1971): 15–17.
———. "Relevant Subject Headings." *U*L*, no. 1 (November 1971): 11–13.
———. "The Scilken Frontlog System." *U*L*, no. 1 (November 1971): 27–29.
———. "Sesame Street." *U*L*, no. 1 (November 1971): 25.
———. "Shoppers' Cards." *U*L*, no. 1 (November 1971): 3.
———. "Some Thoughts on Weeding." *U*L*, no. 1 (November 1971): 24–25.
———. "System Needles Record Loss." *U*L*, no. 1 (November 1971): 23.
———. "Ordering Books by Title." *U*L*, no. 2 (February 1972): 3.
———. "A Public Library Phonorecord System." *U*L*, no. 2 (February 1972): 10–11.
———. "Rush Form." *U*L*, no. 2 (February 1972): 17.
———. "For Two Bits." *U*L*, no. 3 (Spring 1972): 14–15.
———. "Lost in (Catalog) Space." *U*L*, no. 3 (Spring 1972): 3.
———. "'Round Robin' Interlibrary Loan Request Letter." *U*L*, no. 3 (Spring 1972): 24–25.
———. "Two Part Reserve Form." *U*L*, no. 3 (Spring 1972): 13.
———. "Libraries for an Age of Exploration (A Reader Interest Approach)," *U*L*, no. 3 (Spring 1972): 26.
———. "A 'See Also' Card in the Charles Joyce Style." *U*L*, no. 4 (Summer 1972): 10.
———. "CIP to the Readers." *U*L*, no. 4 (Summer 1972): 3.
———. "Measuring Book Activity." *U*L*, no. 4 (Summer 1972): 15.
———. "Relevant Subject Headings." *U*L*, no. 4 (Summer 1972): 21.
———. "Special Fiction Catalog Cards for Saving Typists' Time." *U*L*, no. 4 (Summer 1972): 10.
———. "Tracings at the Top." *U*L*, no. 4 (Summer 1972): 19.
———. "The True Story of Popular Magazines." *U*L*, no. 4 (Summer 1972): 23–25.
———. "Discounts on 'Remainders.'" *U*L*, no. 6 (Winter 1973): 5–6.

―――. "Hardened IBM Typewriter Keys." *U*L*, no. 6 (Winter 1973): 17.

―――. "./=[s.l.][s.n.][s.l.:s.n.] circa p.300 ill. [et al.]." *U*L*, no. 6 (Winter 1973): 21.

―――. "Publishers' 'Net Price' Library Editions." *U*L*, no. 6 (Winter 1973): 29–32.

―――. "Postscript." *U*L*, no. 7 (Spring 1973): 13.

―――. "A Proposed Numerical Union Catalog for Sound Recordings." *U*L*, no. 7 (Spring 1973): 23–24.

―――. "The Read and Return Collection: A Scheme for Overcoming Librarians' Reluctance to Buy Multiple Copies of Popular Books." *U*L*, no. 7 (Spring 1973): 12–13.

―――. "Relevant Subject Headings." *U*L*, no. 7 (Spring 1973): 11.

―――. "Discouraging 'T' Card Switching." *U*L*, no. 8 (Summer 1973): 17.

―――. ". . . Or Try Nixon's Number." *U*L*, no. 8 (Summer 1973): 4.

―――. "How We Use the 'Always Available Book System.'" *U*L*, no. 9 (Fall 1973): 18–21.

―――. "CIP vs. COP." *U*L*, no. 10 (Winter 1974): 31–32.

―――. "Dewey Decimal Impeachment Numbers." *U*L*, no. 11 (Spring 1974): 23.

―――. "The Orange Public Library Subject Inquiry Form." *U*L*, no. 11 (Spring 1974): 22.

―――. "'Win Your Favorite Record' Drawing Designed to Build Record Collection." *U*L*, no. 11 (Spring 1974): 10.

―――. "Children's Books—Binding Costs and Profits." *U*L*, no. 12 (Summer 1974): 26–27.

―――. "Scilken's Super Card." *U*L*, no. 12 (Summer 1974): 32.

―――. "ISBD(M) Arrives." *U*L*, no. 13 (Fall 1974): 16.

―――. "Union 'Catalog' Coding to Encourage Lateral Borrowing." *U*L*, no. 13 (Fall 1974): 15.

―――. "'WIN': Whip Inflation Now. Fight Inflation With Information." *U*L*, no. 13 (Fall 1974): 19.

―――. "Editor's Notes and Ramblings." *U*L*, no. 15 (Spring 1975): 3.

―――. "Scilken's Super Card." *U*L*, no. 15 (Spring 1975): 8.

―――. "Super Card Notes from the Editor." *U*L*, no. 15 (Spring 1975): 13.

―――. "Unpublished Letter to the *Times*." *U*L*, no. 15 (Spring 1975): 13.

―――. "Back to Nature's Light." *U*L*, no. 18 (Winter 1976): 32.

―――. "A Case Against the International Standard Book Number (ISBN)." *U*L*, no. 18 (Winter 1976): 17.

―――. "Coping with a Popular Record Collection." *U*L*, no. 18 (Winter 1976): 31.

―――. "More on What to Do with Books That Fall Apart." *U*L*, no. 18 (Winter 1976): 14.

―――. "Postal Service to Bar 3" x 5" Mail in Two Years." *U*L*, no. 19 (Spring 1976): 28.

―――. "The Cover." *U*L*, no. 22 (1977): 3.

―――. "'Novelizations.'" *U*L*, no. 22 (1977): 16.

―――. "Airplane Type Restrooms for Libraries." *U*L*, no. 26 (1978): 32.

―――. "Another Postal Woe." *U*L*, no. 27 (1978): 25.

———. "Book Jacket Request Postcard." *U*L*, no. 27 (1978): 13.
———. "Library Rate Formula." *U*L*, no. 27 (1978): 25.
———. "Overdue Offer." *U*L*, no. 27 (1978): 25.
———. "Save Your Ball Points." *U*L*, no. 27 (1978): 24.
———. "[Letter to New Jersey Governor Brendan Byrne]." *U*L*, no. 28 (1978): 17.
———. "New Library Rate Formula (As of July 1978)." *U*L*, no. 28 (1978): 5.
———. "Manage Time: Do It Now!" *U*L*, no. 28 (1978): 19.
———. "Random Selection of Stocks and Books." *U*L*, no. 28 (1978): 8.
———. "In Re: x Harold Robbins." *U*L*, no. 29 (1978): 3–4.
———. "Let's Put Some Realism in Public Library Public Relations." *U*L*, no. 30 (1979): 11–12.
———. "'See Also' Cards." *U*L*, no. 30 (1979): 32.
———. "Some Arguments for Public Library Funding in an Urban Area." *U*L*, no. 30 (1979): 28.
———. "More on Dewey 19." *U*L*, no. 32 (1979): 4.
———. "Tail Wags Dog Again and Again." *U*L*, no. 32 (1979): 18.
———. "Speaking to a Group—Use a Written Test." *U*L*, no. 33 (1979): 10.
———. "Children's Book Discounts—Are You Getting Ripped Off?" *U*L*, no. 35 (1980): 3.
———. "Letter to *Publishers Weekly*." *U*L*, no. 35 (1980): 12.
———. "Rental Collection Pays Off." *U*L*, no. 35 (1980): 15.
———. "Better Binding." *U*L*, no. 37 (1980): 25.
———. "Getting Stray Puzzle Pieces to Proper Box." *U*L*, no. 37 (1980): 4.
———. "Some Possible Ways to Differentiate Trade, Publishers' Library Bindings, and Single Reinforced Editions." *U*L*, no. 37 (1980): 13.
———. "Changing Subject Headings." *U*L*, no. 40 (1981): 24.
———. "Stated Messages for Press Releases." *U*L*, no. 41 (1981): 27.
———. "'Stock'ing Books." *U*L*, no. 41 (1981): 32.
———. "Do You Know, Can You Guess?" *U*L*, no. 42 (1982): 8.
———. "Freight Pass Through." *U*L*, no. 46 (1983): 3.
———. "N.t." *U*L*, no. 46 (1983): 28.
———. "Still More." *U*L*, no. 49 (1983): 5–6.
———. "The Medium Size Public Library." *U*L*, no. 50 (1984): 27–29.
———. "Suggestions to Library Book Reviewing Journals." *U*L*, no. 51 (1984): 32.
———. "Thought for This Issue." *U*L*, no. 64 (1987): 15.
———. "Source for 'Real People' Cataloging." *U*L*, no. 68 (1988): 31.
———. "In Case You Never Thought About It." *U*L*, no. 69 (1988): 6.
———. "The Read and Return Collection: A Scheme for Overcoming Librarians' Reluctance to Buy Multiple Copies of Popular Books." *U*L*, no. 72 (1989): 11–12.
———. "'Read the Book' Labels for Videos." *U*L*, no. 72 (1989): 5.
———. "Library Book Reviews: More Information Needed." *U*L*, no. 73 (1989): 10.
———. "A Plea to Mayor Dinkins." *U*L*, no. 74 (1990): 28.

————. "Convention Planner for Indecisive Attendees." *U*L*, no. 75 (1990): 22–23.

————. "Fax Fade." *U*L*, no. 76 (1990): 4.

————. "Recommended Author on the Middle East." *U*L*, no. 76 (1990): 14.

————. "The Cover: Library Users and Voting." *U*L*, no. 77 (1990): 3–4.

————. "For Conference Planners." *U*L*, no. 77 (1990): 11.

————. "[Photocopies of Selected Scilken Letters Published in Various General Interest Magazines]." *U*L*, no. 78 (1991): [37–38].

————. "[Scilken runs for ALA president]." *U*L*, no. 78 (1991): [1–2].

————. "Some Reasons to Vote for Marvin H. Scilken for ALA President." *U*L*, no. 78 (1991): [33].

————. "Classify to 'Merchandise'." *U*L*, no. 79 (1991): 11.

————. "Letter Written to Paul E. Tsongas, Presidential Candidate." *U*L*, no. 79 (1991): 4.

————. "Some Random, Rambling Thoughts on Judge Sarokin's Decision." *U*L*, no. 79 (1991): 17.

————. "Editor's Mumblings: *Libraries Should Focus on Books, Reading, and Literacy*." *U*L*, 80 (1991): 2.

————. "Book Displays Begin in the Middle." *U*L*, no. 80 (1991): 23.

————. "Libraries: Infrastructure of the Mind." *U*L*, no. 83 (1992): [1].

————. "A Letter Written to Principals." *U*L*, no. 84 (1992): 31.

————. "'Sell More of What Sells'—Backlist Books." *U*L*, no. 84 (1992): 14.

————. "How to Determine Whether You've Entered Virtual Reality." *U*L*, no. 85 (1992): 32.

————. "Indiana's Public Library Access Card (PLAC) Program (Statewide Library Card Program)." *U*L*, no. 86 (1993): 23.

————. "College Students in the Public Library: A Letter to the Editor of *New Jersey Libraries*." *U*L*, no. 87 (1993): 21–22.

————. "Letter to a Legislator." *U*L*, no. 87 (1993): 26.

————. "Book Review [of Sharon L. Baker's *The Responsive Public Library Collection: How to Develop and Market It*]." *U*L*, no. 88 (1993): 20.

————. "How to Affect the Legislature." *U*L*, no. 88 (1993): 19.

————. "How Young Pleasure-Seekers at the Library Wind Up Literate." *U*L*, no. 88 (1993): 32.

————. "The Library as Main Street's Ally." *U*L*, no. 89 (1993): 32.

————. "[Review of Marty and Anna Rabkin's] *Public Libraries: Travel Treasures of the West*." *U*L*, no. 89 (1993): 24.

————. "Comparing Per Capita Cost of Municipal Services May Help Libraries." *U*L*, no. 90 (1994): 12.

————. "[Letter on literacy]." *U*L*, no. 90 (1994): 8.

————. "More Mumblings: Public Library Funding." *U*L*, no. 90 (1994): 3–4.

————. "Attendance Comparisons May Help Libraries." *U*L*, no. 91 (1994): 4.

————. "[Letter to the Reader's Digest Association]." *U*L*, no. 91 (1994): 4–5.

————. "More Mumblings (Two Letters)." *U*L*, no. 91 (1994): 7–8.

————. "Classify to 'Merchandise.'" *U*L*, no. 92 (1994): 23.

————. "Culturgrams." *U*L*, no. 92 (1994): 32.

————. "Cuomo Blew It." *U*L*, no. 92 (1994): 23.

————. "Langston Hughes." *U*L*, no. 92 (1994): 24.

138 Holly M. King

———. "The Library Provides." *U*L*, no. 92 (1994): 19.
———. "The Modern World Is Not Dying For Want of Information." *U*L*, no. 94 (1995): 30.
———. "Dover Thrift Editions." *U*L*, no. 95 (1995): 27–29.
———. "Two Letters to the Editor of the *New York Times* (Newt Division)." *U*L*, no. 95 (1995): 7.
———. "Classifying O.J. Simpson Books." *U*L*, no. 96 (1995): 5.
———. "Postcard Used to Solicit Material." *U*L*, no. 96 (1995): 29.
———. "Two Sentences that Public Librarians Should Include in Every Not-For-Publication Letter to a Print Editor." *U*L*, no. 97 (1995): 4.
———. "ALA Conference 'Exhibits Only' Passes." *U*L*, no. 98 (1996): 10.
———. "Building a Book Bandwagon." *U*L*, no. 98 (1996): 21–22.
———. "New York Theater Ticket Hints." *U*L*, no. 98 (1996): 29.
———. "Tax Facts??" *U*L*, no. 98 (1996): 4.
———. "Better Libraries." *U*L*, no. 100 (1996): 7–8.
———. "Libraries as Active Disseminators of Truth." *U*L*, no. 100 (1996): 26.
———. "Woo Non-Users as Supporters." *U*L*, no. 100 (1996): 11–12.
———. "Keep Your Fax On." *U*L*, no. 101 (1996): 26.
———. "Letter on HarperCollins Book Discounts." *U*L*, no. 101 (1996): 21.
———. "A Letter to *Harper's* Magazine on 'Silence, Please: The Public Library as Entertainment Center'." *U*L*, no. 101 (1996): 15–16.
———. "Dewey for the 21st Century." *U*L*, no. 102 (1997): 9.
———. "Gift Book Thoughts." *U*L*, no. 102 (1997): 11.
———. "Letter to the Editor on 'America Reads'." *U*L*, no. 102 (1997): 4.
———. "Library-Boosting Letters Rewarded." *U*L*, no. 102 (1997): 4.
———. "The Basketball Court of Reading." *U*L*, no. 103 (1997): 18.
———. "Letter to New Jersey's New Governor." *U*L*, no. 103 (1997): 31.
———. "Library-Boosting Letters Rewarded." *U*L*, no. 103 (1997): 10.
———. "More Mumblings: A Response to an Editorial in *Public Libraries*." *U*L*, no. 103 (1997): 12.
———. "Publishers Join First Lady's Literacy Initiative." *U*L*, no. 103 (1997): 28.
———. "Library Checks." *U*L*, no. 104 (1997): 8.
———. "About Staples (Not the Store)." *U*L*, no. 105 (1997): 22.
———. "Children Need Incentive to Get Them to Read." *U*L*, no. 105 (1997): 14.
———. "Classification of Books Is Very Important." *U*L*, no. 105 (1997): 28.
———. "It's Bad Politics to Cut the Library Budget." *U*L*, no. 105 (1997): 18.
———. "Letter to Anthony Lewis." *U*L*, no. 105 (1997): 8.
———. "Letters We All Should Be Writing." *U*L*, no. 105 (1997): 8.
———. "Monopoly Position Allows for Imposition of OPACs." *U*L*, no. 105 (1997): 20.
———. "My Novel 'Vanished Entirely Off the Planet'." *U*L*, no. 105 (1997): 22.
———. "The Original Letter to the *New York Times*." *U*L*, no. 105 (1997): 10.
———. "Philadelphia's Public-Private Effort." *U*L*, no. 107 (1998): 25–26.
———. "Retrieving Overdues—Some Thoughts." *U*L*, no. 107 (1998): 4–5.

———. "Write On." *U*L*, no. 107 (1998): 12.
———. "Jeopardy/Library Connection (A Letter)." *U*L*, no. 108 (1998): 9.
———. "Location Is Everything." *U*L*, no. 108 (1998): 31.
———. "One Solution to the Test Practice Book Problem." *U*L*, no. 108 (1998): 10–11.
———. "Perhaps an Easy Way to Survey Customer Satisfaction." *U*L*, no. 108 (1998): 20.
———. "Reading Slogans at Times Square?" *U*L*, no. 108 (1998): 30.
———. "Shelving Genre Fiction." *U*L*, no. 109 (1998): 9.
———. "Backlog to Frontlog: A Scheme for Circulating Nonfiction Books Without the Help of the Library of Congress." *U*L*, no. 110 (1999): 20–21.
———. "A Visit to Brooklyn's Brighton Beach Branch." *U*L*, no. 110 (1999): 26–27.
———. "Getting New Adult Steady Users." *U*L*, no. 111 (1999): 29.
———. "A Plea for Children's Library Binding Standards." *U*L*, no. 111 (1999): 17.
———. "Publishers' Subsidy." *U*L*, no. 111 (1999): 15.
———. "Letters We All Should Be Writing." *U*L*, no. 112 (1999): 27.
———. "Libraries: Infrastructure of the Mind." *U*L*, no. 112 (1999): [1].
———. "Philosophy." *U*L*, no. 113 (1999): 2.
———. "College Students in the Public Library." *U*L*, no. 113 (1999): 7–11.

Other Publications

Scilken, Marvin H. "Reference Service to Adults." *Odds and Book Ends* no. 36 (Fall 1960): 104–5.
———. "Backlog to Frontlog: A Scheme for Circulating Nonfiction Books Without the Help of the Library of Congress." *Library Journal* 94, no. 16 (15 September 1969): 3014–15.
———. "The Read and Return Collection: A Scheme for Overcoming Librarians' Reluctance to Buy Multiple Copies of Popular Books." *Wilson Library Bulletin* 46, no. 1 (September 1971): 104–5.
———. "Realism in Public Library Public Relations." *Library Journal* 97, no. 7 (1 April 1972): 1246–47.
———. "Cataloging Time-Lag [Review of S. Elspeth Pope's *The Time-Lag in Cataloging*]." *Library Journal* 98, no. 18 (15 October 1973): 2982.
———. "Let's Try COP." *Library Journal* 99, no. 18 (15 October 1974): 2582–83.
———. "Make Your Point: Business Cents." *School Library Journal* 21, no. 3 (November 1974): 38.
———. "Make Your Point: Business Cents." *Library Journal* 99, no. 20 (15 November 1974): 3028.
———. "The Morality of Reciprocal Borrowing." *New Jersey Libraries* 8, no. 1 (January 1975): 10, 12.

———. "Demystifying the Catalogue." *Emergency Librarian* 4, no. 4 (March/April 1977): 3–5.

———. "Demystifying the Catalogue." in *Library Lit. 8—The Best of 1977*, ed. Bill Katz (Metuchen, N.J.: Scarecrow, 1978), 147–151.

———. "Food for Thought: Orange Public Library Rental Collection." *New Jersey Libraries* 11, no. 4 (June 1978): 24–25.

———. "The Catalog as a Public Service Tool," in *The Nature and Future of the Catalog: Proceedings of the ALA's Information Science and Automation Division's 1975 and 1977 Institutes on the Catalog*, ed. Maurice J. Freedman and S. Michael Malinconico (Phoenix: Oryx Press, 1979), 89–101.

———. "My Say." *Publishers Weekly* 225, no. 22 (1 June 1984): 60.

———. "Forum: Public Relations for Public Libraries Usually Misdirected." *Canadian Library Journal* 46, no. 5 (October 1989): 352.

———. "Breaking the Bind: Net Pricing Scandal of Publishers' Library Bindings." *School Library Journal* 36, no. 3 (March 1990): 160.

———. "The New Jersey State Library." *New Jersey Libraries* 29, no. 4 (Winter 1996): 34.

Selected Letters

Scilken, Marvin H. "[Cuts in New York City library budgets]." *New York Times*, 6 May 1969, 46.

———. "[Reply to J.B. Rhoades]." *New York Times*, 12 October 1969, 25(7).

———. "LC Card Game." *American Libraries* 1, no. 7 (July 1970): 650–51.

———. "Completing the State Library's Public Library Statistics Report Prompts a Few Suggestions and Comments." *New Jersey Libraries* 3, no. 4 (Winter 1970): 34–35.

———. "Cataloging for 'Real' People." *Library Journal* 98, no. 12 (15 June 1973): 1856–57.

———. "On Binding Practices." *School Library Journal* 20, no. 6 (February 1974): 3.

———. "On Binding Practices." *Library Journal* 99, no. 4 (15 February 1974): 513.

———. "[Vanity presses and subsidized publications of specialized corporate books]." *New York Times*, 16 November 1975, 9(3).

———. "'A Disinterested Horse'." *Library Journal* 102, no. 6 (15 March 1977): 645.

———. "Sound Off!" *NYLA Bulletin* 25, no. 4 (April 1977): 9.

———. "Whither 'Grown-Ups'?" *Wilson Library Bulletin* 52, no. 2 (October 1977): 128, 130.

———. "Serving a Greedy Few." *American Libraries* 8, no. 11 (December 1977): 599.

———. "Of Spineless Books." *Wilson Library Bulletin* 52, no. 9 (May 1978): 689.

———. "The 47% Introductory Discount Ad." *Publishers Weekly* 214, no. 18 (30 October 1978): 9.

———. "[State library aid]." *New Jersey Libraries* 12, no. 3 (April 1979): 26–27.

———. "Prefers Jarvis to Seymour." *American Libraries* 10, no. 8 (September 1979): 457.

———. "[Reply to New Jersey Library Association]." *New Jersey Libraries* 12, no. 8 (December 1979): 28.

———. "Bound for ALA." *School Library Journal* 26, no. 8 (April 1980): 4.

———. "[Reply to M. Gorman and J. Hotsinpiller]." *College and Research Libraries* 41, no. 3 (May 1980): 245.

———. "DDC 19: This Mess." *Library Journal* 105, no. 11 (1 June 1980): 1240.

———. "[Fees for public library service]." *New Jersey Libraries* 13, no. 5 (September 1980): 40–41.

———. "Library Binding Prices." *Library Journal* 105, no. 15 (1 September 1980): 1675.

———. "Emphasizing Primary Services." *Wilson Library Bulletin* 55, no. 3 (November 1980): 167.

———. "Reading's the Best Way." *Newark Star-Ledger*, 4 December 1988.

———. "Core Curriculum: Other Options." *New York Times*, 19 February 1989, 26(12NJ).

———. "Save the Penny." *New York Times*, 24 March 1989, 30(1).

———. "Turning Children into Readers." *New York Times*, 13 August 1989, 18(12NJ).

———. "How Libraries Fight Crime." *New York Newsday*, 21 September 1990.

———. "[Equalization aid for New Jersey public libraries]." *New York Times*, 14 October 1990, 20(12NJ).

———. "An Open Book Is an Invitation to Joy." *Wall Street Journal*, 25 October 1990.

———. "Book Smart." *New York*, 26 November 1990.

———. "Letter Written to Paul E. Tsongas, Presidential Candidate." *U*L* no. 79 (1991): 4.

———. "Out of Print? Don't Forget the Library." *Business Week*, 18 March 1991, 13.

———. "The Car Buyer's Edge." *New York Times*, 29 May 1991, 22(A).

———. "Misguided Zeal Turns Libraries Into Shelters." *Wall Street Journal*, 23 December 1991.

———. "Libraries and Cooking." *New York Times*, 26 February 1992, 8(C).

———. "Libraries: Infrastructure of the Mind." *Newark Star-Ledger*, 30 March 1992.

———. "AIDS Education Costs." *New York Times*, 19 May 1992, 22(A).

———. "Reading for Pleasure, Not Just for Tests." *New York Times*, 4 October 1992, 16(4).

———. "How to Determine Whether You've Entered Virtual Reality." *Business Week*, 16 November 1992, 7.

———. "One More Kudo for Bell Atlantic." *New York Times*, 21 March 1993, 11(3).

————. "Libraries." *New York Times*, 27 June 1993, 10(10).
————. "ALA Gets Practical." *Library Journal* 118, no. 15 (15 September 1993): 8, 10.
————. "How Young Pleasure-seekers at the Library Wind Up Literate." *New York Times*, 27 September 1993, 16(A).
————. "The Library as Main Street's Ally." *New York Times*, 14 November 1993, 11 (3).
————. "[Literacy]." *Newark Star-Ledger*, 4 February 1994.
————. "Providing What Customers Want," *Public Libraries* 33, no. 2 (March/April 1994): 119.
————. "A Response to an Editorial," *Public Libraries* 33, no. 5 (September/October 1994): 286.
————. "[Letter to James P. Schadt]." *U*L* no. 91 (1994), 5.
————. "To the Editor of *Public Libraries*." *U*L* no. 91 (1994), 7.
————. "Langston Hughes." *Smithsonian* 25, no. 7 (October 1994): 10.
————. "The Library Provides." *New York Times*, 13 October 1994, 26(A).
————. "Libraries Aid New Authors by Holding Onto Books." *New York Times*, 30 October 1994, 12(13).
————. "Library Postal Increase." *New York Times*, 5 January 1995, 26(A).
————. "Don't Forget About American Coat Makers." *New York Times*, 5 February 1995, 11(B).
————. ". . . And More Exceptional in Queens than Manhattan." *New York Times*, 27 August 1995, 15(13CY).
————. "Literacy's Missing Link." *School Library Journal* 42, no. 3 (March 1996): 92.
————. "Dear Editor." *U*L* no. 98 (1996): 22.
————. "Better Libraries." *Newark Star-Ledger*, 6 November 1996.
————. "Brain Food for Babies." *Time*, 149, no. 8 (24 February 1997): 10.
————. "Check Them Out!" *Library Journal* 22 15 (15 September 1997): 8.
————. "Renovated Library Is a Paradigm." *New York Times*, 21 November 1998, 14(A).
————. "Speaking Volumes." *American Way*, 32, no. 7 (1 April 1999): 12.

Publications About Marvin Scilken by Other Authors

"Pratt Profile: Marvin H. Scilken." *Pratt Alumnus* (August 1966).
Subcommittee on Antitrust and Monopoly of the Committee on the Judiciary. *Alleged Price Fixing on Library Books: Hearings on S. Res. 191.* 89th Congress, 2nd sess., March 23, 24 and May 12, 1966. Washington, D.C.: U.S. Government Printing Office, 1966.
"Library Front-Liners: Marvin Scilken, Library Consumer Advocate." *Wilson Library Bulletin* 46, no. 8 (April 1972): 692–93.
Johnson Jr., Pyke. "What Publishers Should Know About the Public Library . . . A Book Editor's Firsthand Report." *Publishers Weekly* 211, no. 13 (28 March 1977): 40–42.

Mouat, Lucia. "Budget-Pinched Libraries Try to Give Patrons More of What They Want." *Christian Science Monitor*, 3 June 1980, 4.

"Rotarian Librarian." *Rotarian*, 144 (June 1984), 47.

Deitch, Joseph. "Portrait: Marvin Scilken." *Wilson Library Bulletin* 59, no. 3 (November 1984): 205–7.

Gertzog, Alice. "Library Leaders: Who and Why?" *Library Journal* 115, no. 12 (July 1990): 45–51.

Deitch, Joseph. "Portrait: Marvin." *U*L* no. 78 (1991): 34–36.

"Four ALA Candidates Address Chicago Midwinter." *School Library Journal* 37, no. 2 (February 1991): 12.

"ALA Candidates Speak Their Minds in April *Library Journal*." *School Library Journal* 37, no. 4 (April 1991): 17.

"ALA Candidates on ACRL," *College and Research Libraries News* 52, no. 4 (April 1991): 244.

"ALA Candidates: Why Choose?" *Library Journal* 116, no. 6 (1 April 1991): 74–82.

"'Why Should I Vote for You?' ALA Presidential Candidates Respond." *American Libraries* 22, no. 5 (May 1991): 454–55.

Mouat, Lucia. "Libraries Feel the Pinch in Tough Economic Times." *Christian Science Monitor*, 17 July 1991, 9.

"Marvin H. Scilken to Retire." *Region 3 Information Plus* 6 (Spring 1993): 1.

"Library World." *Wilson Library Bulletin* 67, no. 8 (April 1993): 27.

"People." *Library Journal* 118, no. 6 (1 April 1993): 40.

"Currents." *American Libraries* 24, no. 5 (May 1993): 432.

Berry III, John N. "ALA's Agenda: Let's Get On with It!" *Library Journal* 118, no. 12 (July 1993): 6.

Robinson, Regan, "Selection with Scilken." *Librarians Collection Letter: A Monthly Newsletter for Collection Development Staff* 5, no. 2 (July 1998): 1, 3, 6.

Schneider, Karen G. "Desperately Seeking Marvin." *American Libraries* 28, no. 6 (June/July 1997): 116.

Scilken, Mary P. "Mumblings About and From the Editor." *U*L* no. 110 (1999): 3.

"Deaths." *New York Times*, 5 February 1999, 11(B).

"Deaths." *New York Times*, 8 February 1999, 8(B).

"Obituaries." *Publishers Weekly* 246, no. 6 (8 February 1999): 104.

"Publisher, PL Director Scilken Dies Attending ALA Midwinter." *Library Hotline* 28, no. 5 (8 February 1999): 1.

"Deaths." *New York Times*, 18 February 1999, 23(C).

Robinson, Regan, "Collection Wisdom from Marvin Scilken." *Librarians Collection Letter: A Monthly Newsletter for Collection Development Staff* 8, no. 9 (February 1999): 1, 6.

Eberhart, George, Gordon Flagg, and Leonard Kniffel. "Feting Freedoms in Philadelphia: The Death of a Colleague Solemnifies ALA's Midwinter Celebration of Its Most Enduring Values." *American Libraries* 30, no. 3 (March 1999): 68–74.

Kniffel, Leonard. "Death Is Never on the Agenda." *American Libraries* 30, no. 3 (March 1999): 34.

"One of the Very Unfortunate Events at ALA." *SCLC Review* 21, no. 3 (March 1999): 1.

"Outsourcing Debate Dominates, Boy Scouts Chided." *American Libraries* 30, no. 3 (March 1999): 83–85.

"Tributes to Marvin Scilken (December 7, 1926–February 3, 1999)." *American Libraries* 30, no. 3 (March 1999): 84.

"Unabashed Librarian Marvin Scilken Dies at ALA Midwinter." *American Libraries* 30, no. 3 (March 1999): 89.

Rogers, Michael, and Norman Oder. "ALA Holds Midwinter Amid Revelry Laced with Tragedy." *Library Journal* 124, no. 4 (1 March 1999): 12–13.

———. "Popular Scilken Dies Suddenly in Philly." *Library Journal* 124, no. 4 (1 March 1999): 13.

Schneider, Karen G. "The Elements of Marvin." *American Libraries* 30, no. 4 (April 1999): 88.

Scilken, Polly, and Sanford Berman. "Remembering Marvin." *American Libraries* 30, no. 4 (April 1999): 37.

Zyroff, Ellen, and Jack Forman. "Will Marvin's Legacy Be Placed in Jeopardy?" *American Libraries* 30, no. 5 (May 1999): 40.

"Marvin Scilken," *STLS Currents* (May/June 1999): 14.

"100 of the Most Important Leaders We Had in the 20th Century." *American Libraries* 30, no. 11 (December 1999): 38–46, 48.

Scilken, Mary P. "From the Editor." *U*L* no. 113 (1999): 3.

"New *Unabashed Librarian* Named." *American Libraries* 31, no. 2 (February 2000): 21.

Index

About the Contributors

Lisa Bier is currently employed as Social Sciences Reference Librarian at Southern Connecticut State University in New Haven, Connecticut. She received a Master's of Library and Information Science degree from the University of Texas at Austin in 1998.

Antony Cherian is a graduate student at the University of Texas at Austin. He has done time in public libraries on three continents. Working on Marvin Scilken's festschrift has helped ease his conscience of losing that library book on crocodiles when he was six years old.

For **Joseph Deitch**, libraries held a central place in a six decade-long career as writer, public relations director, and journalist. Mr. Deitch wrote dozens of articles on libraries, librarians, books, and information for the *Wilson Library Bulletin*, including a profile of Marvin Scilken. After serving in the U.S. Army during World War II—he wrote and edited the base newspaper at Fort Sam Houston, Texas—he began his professional career as a special correspondent for the *Christian Science Monitor* while attending Columbia University. In 1949 he became Public Information Officer of Teachers College, Columbia University, a position he held for fifteen years. He directed public relations and public affairs departments at Lincoln Center for the Performing Arts, Cornell University Medical College, the United Federation of Teachers, the Municipal Services Administration of the City of New York, the Polytechnic Institute of New York, and Rutgers University in Newark, among other positions. He loved working at academic institutions, in part because they provided access to great libraries. As a freelance journalist, Mr. Deitch wrote hundreds of articles for the *New York Times* and many other publications. He died in December 2001, leaving his wife Edna, two sons, two grandsons, and a sprawling personal library.

Katherine A. Flowers is currently pursuing a Master's degree in the Graduate School of Library and Information Science at the University of Texas at Austin. She holds a Bachelor of Arts from Texas A&M University and has taught high school English and Reading. Her areas of interest are readers' advisory and the public library. She currently works at the Westbank Community Library in Austin, Texas.

Jack Forman is a librarian at the San Diego Mesa College Library in San Diego, California, a public community college serving twenty-three thousand students. At the present time, he serves as the chair of the college's Learning Resource Center (LRC) and oversees the library's public services program and circulation services. He holds degrees from the University of Rochester and Rutgers University. His reviews of books currently appear in *Library Journal*, *School Library Journal*, *The Horn Book Guide* and *Reference Books Bulletin* (*Booklist* Magazine), and he has written book reviews in the past for newspaper book sections of the *San Diego Union* and the *New York Times*. In addition, he is the author of *Presenting Paul Zindel*, a bio-critical study of the playwright and young-adult novelist. He also is active in the American Library Association (ALA) and the California Library Association (CLA). He has served two terms on the ALA Council and he currently serves on many ALA and divisional committees. He also serves as the Academic Libraries section representative in the CLA Assembly and is a member of CLA committees. Forman first met Marvin H. Scilken when they were colleagues at different public libraries in northern New Jersey, and he re-established contact with him when Scilken served as his Council mentor during Forman's first elected term on ALA Council in 1986.

Joanna F. Fountain has been a lecturer in beginning and advanced courses in cataloging and classification (Organization of Materials) for the Graduate School of Library and Information Science at the University of Texas at Austin since 1990, and online for Western Maryland College since 1999. As an independent librarian and consultant she has been the Database Administrator for the Texas Education Agency's Texas Library Connection project since 1998, has conducted numerous workshops each year and cataloged materials on a contract basis for school and special libraries. She previously worked in school, public, special, and academic libraries. Her degrees include a B.A. in Spanish and Library Science from Syracuse University, 1966, a M.L.S. from the University of Texas at Austin, 1970, and the Ph.D. in Library Science from Texas Woman's University, 1982. Dr. Fountain's most recent publication is the third edition of *Subject Headings for School and Public Libraries* (2001). Earlier publications include two editions of the multicultural bibliography *Hey, Miss! You got a book for Me?*, directories and bibliographies related to bilingual and multicultural education and academic special collections, and numerous reviews in international journals.

Maurice ("Mitch") J. Freedman is director of the Westchester (New York) Library System, a position he has held since 1982, a cooperative library system of fifty-eight public libraries serving a population of 875,000. He received an

MLS degree from the University of California, Berkeley and a Ph.D. from Rutgers University. He is the current editor and publisher of the *U*N*A*B*A*S*H*E*D Librarian*. He is widely known as an author, consultant, and as the American Library Association President-Elect, 2001–2002.

Holly M. King is pursuing an MLIS at the Graduate School of Library and Information Science at the University of Texas at Austin. Her studies have focused on library science and reference services. Before entering graduate school, she worked for several years as an editor. King received a BA in English and history from Southwestern University, where she is currently serving as an intern in the Reference and Special Collections departments of the university's Smith Library Center.

Matthew Mantel is currently a reference librarian at the Jacob Burns Law Library, the George Washington University School of Law. He received a BA in History from the University of Texas at Austin and a JD degree from South Texas College of Law in Houston, Texas where he practiced law from 1994–1999. He received a Masters in Library and Information Science from the University of Texas at Austin in May 2001.

Dan O'Connor is an associate professor in the Department of Library and Information Science at Rutgers where he teaches research methods in the undergraduate, master's, and doctoral programs at the School of Communication, Information, and Library Studies. He holds Ph.D. and MSLS degrees from Syracuse University. He has worked as a reference librarian and as a cataloger/head of technical services. Currently, O'Connor is the digital projects consultant for the Digital Picture Collection federally funded project at New York Public Library's Mid-Manhattan Library. O'Connor has served as a consultant to the Conference Board, the Metropolitan Museum of Art, and to numerous libraries. Dan has served as President of Rutgers' American Association of University Professors (AAUP), the faculty union, and has served as chief negotiator for the Rutgers AAUP Collective Bargaining Contract. Currently, he is president of the New Jersey State Conference of the AAUP representing over eight thousand faculty at ten higher education institutions. Dan first met Marvin Scilken in 1974 when he joined the Rutgers faculty. Scilken was a driving intellectual force on the New Jersey Library Association's Library Development Committee, which O'Connor chaired for a number of years in the 1980s and 1990s. A number of Scilken's ideas were implemented by this committee.

Regan Robinson is the director of the Stevens County Rural Library District in Loon Lake, Washington. From 1991 until 1999 she published the *Librarians Collection Letter*, a monthly newsletter for collection staff in public libraries. She received her MLS from Simmons College in 1974.

Loriene Roy is a professor in the Graduate School of Library and Information Science at the University of Texas at Austin. She received a Ph.D. from the University of Illinois (1987) and also holds degrees from the University of Arizona and Oregon Institute of Technology. She co-edited *Library and*

Information Studies Education in the United States (1998) and has over one hundred other publications to her credit. Her professional work focuses on library services for indigenous populations. She serves as director of "If I Can Read, I Can Do Anything," a reading promotion program for schools on or near reservations. She teaches graduate courses in public librarianship, reference sources and services in the humanities and social sciences, library instruction, and adult popular fiction. Her research also includes creating a National Virtual Museum of the American Indian, conducting a study of Spectrum Initiative scholars for the American Library Association, and co-developing an intelligent agent for book recommending. She has been active in the American Library Association and was a Councilor-at-Large when she met Marvin S. Scilken in early 1996. She is Anishinabe (Ojibwe), is enrolled on the White Earth Reservation, and is a member of the Minnesota Chippewa Tribe (Pembina Band).

Karen G. Schneider is the assistant director for technology at the Shenendehowa Public Library in Clifton Park, New York. She is active in the American Library Association, having served as a Councilor-at-Large since 1997. She has written extensively on Internet filtering and since June 1995 has written "The Internet Librarian" column for *American Libraries.*

Mary P. Scilken (better known as Polly) is retired from Pace University where she served as associate professor and chairperson of the Nursing Department on the New York City campus. She was a nursing educator for about fifteen years. Prior to that she was in nursing practice, in the field of Community Health, for many years. A graduate of the Indiana University School of Nursing, she continued her education for a BS from Hunter College and an MS and Ph.D. from New York University.

She and Marvin Scilken were married in 1962 and had two sons and two grandsons. She assisted Marvin when he created and published the *U*N*A*B*A*S*H*E*D Librarian*, and she continued its publication for a year following his death in 1999. She is enjoying retirement and lives in New York City in the home she shared with Marvin and their children.

Marjorie Scilken-Friedman, Marvin's older and only sibling, is an investigator of discrimination complaints for the New York District Office of the Equal Employment Opportunity Commission (EEOC), a federal agency.

This role and commitment developed subsequent to an academic career: MA Teachers College, Columbia University; Ph.D. Steinhardt, New York University; and teaching assignments at New York University, City University of New York (CUNY), University of Puerto Rico, and the University of Tel-Aviv. This career came to an end in the 1970s because of active support for minority representation during demonstrations and sit-ins at CUNY.

Peggy Sullivan, a library consultant specializing in executive searches for public library administrators, lives in Chicago, Illinois. Her work in the American Library Association (ALA) includes three stints as a staff member, most recently executive director of the association (1992–1994), as well as numerous appointive and elective positions in ALA and its various divisions. She served as ALA president in 1980–1981. She holds a Ph.D. from the University of Chicago, an MS in LS from Catholic University of America, and an AB from Clarke College, Dubuque, Iowa. Her library career included work in public libraries, school libraries, and library education.